Ebay Seller Secrets!

Tips & Tricks to Increase Your Sales & Make More Money

By
Ann Eckhart

Table of Contents

INTRODUCTION

I began my Ebay selling career in 2005 when I was trying to liquidate some excess inventory from my home-based gift basket business. I had never sold anything on Ebay prior to that, so I was shocked at how quickly I was able to sell my overstocked items!

After selling my extra gift basket supplies, I cleared out my closets of unwanted clothing and accessories, all of which sold on Ebay quickly and for great prices. I then began searching for more things I could sell online. I discovered that many of my gift basket suppliers also sold stand-alone gifts such as ceramics, plush toys and books. I slowly started ordering those items to sell; and they were such a hit that by the end of the year I had quit the gift basket business and was selling only new gifts on Ebay! I eventually expanded to Amazon, and for a few years my Amazon sales actually outnumbered my Ebay sales 10-1.

As the years wore on, however, the online selling landscape changed. Not only were more and more retailers jumping online themselves, but even the wholesale companies that I ordered from began selling online directly to customers. Before long, I was pushed out of the gift market and had to find another business strategy. Fortunately, I had a back-up plan

From time to time while I was still selling new gifts, I had also purchased things at garage sales and thrift stores to resell on Ebay. When the time came when new gifts were no longer an option for me to resell, I jumped head first into "picking" (or "reselling", as I prefer to call it). My weekends were spent going to every garage sale and estate sale I could find; and my business found new life in selling vintage pieces, collectibles, and clothing

However, regardless of whether I was selling new gifts or secondhand clothing, I always maintained the same level of stellar customer service and business practices. With trial and error, I learned a lot about what worked and what didn't when selling online. In all of my years of selling on Ebay, I have acquired lots of tips and tricks for increasing sales, all of which I am sharing with you in this book!

Too many sellers focus only on sourcing products and making money; but there is a lot that goes into a successful Ebay sale. Ebay is a unique marketplace. You can run auctions or sell items at Fixed Price. You accept payments through PayPal. Customers can leave you feedback that can either boost or destroy your business. However, there are lots of things you can do to make the Ebay selling process go smoothly, resulting in more sales and more money!

From writing listings and taking photographs, to answering customer questions and handling returns, this book is filled with everything I personally know how to do in order to sell successfully on Ebay. These are all things I have done over the years to keep customers happy and to keep growing my sales. All of the advice in this book is straightforward and easy to implement, and I sincerely hope you are able to use these tips and tricks yourself to increase your sales and make more money!

CHAPTER 1

MASTERING THE BASICS OF EBAY

Before we jump into the finer points and details of selling on Ebay, let's first go over some basic skills that every seller needs to have in order to be successful. If you've read any of my other books, you'll recognize these tips; but they are so important that I'm reiterating them here. Even if you've already been selling on Ebay for a while, these points may still help you to improve your business.

These are things that may seem obvious to most people, but you would be surprised as how many times I am asked about selling on Ebay by people who don't possess one or more of these skills or tools. However, it's important that you master these basic skills and have all of the tools you need before you begin selling on Ebay

The Basic Tools: There are three pieces of equipment you must have in order to sell on Ebay, which are a computer, printer and digital camera or smart phone with an excellent camera. You also need to have a strong working knowledge of computers. Now, you don't need to know programming or html code to sell online; but Ebay is an online business that is run via the internet using computers; so not only do you need to be comfortable with the internet, computers, and printers, you also have to actually own these tools in your home.

Having a computer set up may seem completely obvious to most people, but I can't tell you how many times I have been approached by someone asking me about how they can sell on Ebay....without a computer! If you aren't familiar with computers or if you need to brush up on your skills, look for free or low-cost computer classes in your area at the library, community college, or recreational center.

If you don't already have a computer, printer, and/or digital camera/smart phone, start shopping the sales and looking for a basic model; you can get a beginning set up of equipment for anywhere from $500 to $1000. I use a Dell laptop, an HP LaserJet printer, and used to use a Canon point-and-shoot camera; on sale, I could buy all three of these items today for around $700. Today I take all of my Ebay photos with my iPhone.

I pay $50 a month for high-speed internet access. Most phone and cable companies now offer internet services, including modems so that you can have wireless access. Call around to the internet providers in your area and ask about any packages or specials they have for new customers. Be careful about getting locked into a long-term contract, however; and be sure you are aware of any price increases that will take place once the introductory special is over.

Does all of this already sound like too much work or too much money? Remember that selling on Ebay is a business, and in business, you often have to spend money in order to make money. Don't attempt to start reselling online until you are able to acquire the equipment needed.

A computer, printer, internet access, and camera are just some of the tools you need to successfully sell on Ebay. You also need the physical ability to go out and source products, meaning you need a car to get to garage sales and thrift stores. Just like the people who wanted to sell on Ebay without a computer, I've also dealt with people who wanted to be resellers....but had no transportation. I even know someone who attempted to sell on Ebay using the computers and printers at the library, which he got to by hitching rides with family and friends. Needless to say, his Ebay career was short-lived.

A computer, printer, internet access, camera, and transportation will help you buy products and get them listed onto Ebay, but you also need space to store your inventory. I currently have a basement dedicated to my Ebay stock, but at one time I had it all in a spare bedroom. And even if you don't plan on running a full-scale Ebay business, you are going to need a place to keep the items you are selling, whether it's a spare closet or the corner of a room. While most of my Ebay items are in my basement, Ebay inventory and shipping materials tend to find their ways into all parts of my home.

Oh, did I just mention the shipping materials? From boxes and envelopes to tape and packing paper, the supplies you need to keep on hand to ship your Ebay items can easily fill a closet on their own. I actually have four shelving units (5 shelves each) and a desk dedicated to my Ebay shipping supplies.

I also have a separate table in my office for my digital scale as well as a dedicated space set up for taking photographs. I also invest in enclosure cards that go into every package that thank customers for their order. The "stuff" I need to run my Ebay business almost takes up as much space as my inventory!

As you can see, selling on Ebay requires a lot more than just buying products to resell. Be sure you have the tools, skills, and space you need to obtain, list, store, and ship your items. You want your focus to be on making money, not spending time figuring out how to upload photos or finding a place to store shipping boxes.

Your Ebay & PayPal Accounts: In order to sell on Ebay, you need both an Ebay account AND a PayPal account. PayPal is Ebay's payment system; it works like a debit card for buyers. Customers create a PayPal account and connect it to their bank account and/or credit/debit card. When they purchase something on Ebay, the money is paid to the seller directly through PayPal.

This system eliminates the need for sellers to have their own merchant (i.e. credit card processing) accounts, and it also prevents customers and sellers from having to exchange their personal banking information with one another. While PayPal can seem scary to new sellers, it is extremely safe to use and preferable to having to deal with other payments such as checks (when I first started selling on Ebay, it was common practice for sellers to accept checks and money orders via the mail). I have been using PayPal since 2005, and I have never once had any problems with it.

In order to get paid on Ebay, sellers also need to have a PayPal account. PayPal payments can only be made to other PayPal accounts. So, if you are going to sell on Ebay, you MUST create a PayPal account. You will need to back up your PayPal account with a bank account; and even better, a credit card. Your bank account needs to be linked to your PayPal account so that you can withdraw money; and the credit card is a back up to paying your Ebay fees if you don't automatically pay them on your own.

I have both a bank account AND a credit card on file with PayPal. When a customer buys something from me on Ebay, they use PayPal to pay for their purchase. The total amount is deposited into MY PayPal account. From there, I print off the shipping label and the postage cost is taken directly from my PayPal balance. PayPal does charge a small fee, which also comes out from my balance. After I have shipped an item, the remaining balance is all mine and ready to be withdrawn into my bank account.

Since I rarely keep a PayPal balance, having a credit card on file allows me to make my own purchases. If I do make a purchase using PayPal, I usually just have it go through my credit card. However, the person I am buying from only gets the money via PayPal, not my actual credit card. And if I forget to pay my Ebay fees (although I do pay them every few days to avoid a huge balance piling up), the fees are automatically charged to my card at the end of each billing cycle.

To put it simply, PayPal is the middle man who deals with the exchange of money between you and your customers; and you MUST have a PayPal account to sell on Ebay. To set up your Ebay and PayPal accounts, simply go to Ebay.com and click on the "register" link in the upper left-hand corner. Then just follow the easy online instructions to get set up!

UPDATE: Note that in 2019, Ebay began the transition from PayPal to its own Managed Payments system. While existing sellers can still use PayPal for their Ebay business, new users are being enrolled into Managed Payments. Managed Payments works like any other online retailer in that customers pay directly for their purchases on Ebay, bypassing PayPal altogether. Managed Payment is still in its beta phase and won't be fully rolled out to all Ebay users until 2022.

Getting Started: So, you have the computer, internet access, printer, camera, car, space, and shipping supplies; plus, your Ebay and PayPal accounts are all set up. You are ready to jump in to selling on Ebay with both feet, right? Hold it right there! Before SELLING on Ebay, you should do yourself a favor and actually BUY some things on Ebay first.

Ebay is a unique marketplace. You can bid on auctions or buy things at fixed price. You can also send sellers offers. Once you've committed to buying an item, you'll need to pay with PayPal. Every seller sets their own shipping time; so, while some sellers may ship out orders the same day, others may wait a week. Shopping on Ebay is very different than ordering from Amazon or any other online retailer; and you'll learn a lot about Ebay works by actually buying a few things before you starting selling.

There are lots of 99-cent items on Ebay, so you don't have to spend much money during this process of learning how to buy. What you are looking for is experience, not a great deal; find a handful of cheap items to purchase so you can see how Ebay works from the buyer's point of view.

Not only will buying items teach you about the Ebay ordering and PayPal payment processes, but you'll also see how other sellers run their businesses. Do you get notice of your order shipping along with tracking? Does your item arrive in the amount of time promised in the listing? Is your order packed well and with clean packing materials? Was a packing slip included? Is the item you received in the condition it was listed as? What you observe of other seller's practices will greatly help you shape your own.

Once you have become comfortable as an Ebay buyer, it's time to start selling. However, before you run out and buy up a bunch of stuff at the thrift store to resell, look around your own home for some things to sell. DVD's, video games, cookbooks, toys, and clothing you are no longer using will not only bring you in come cash, but listing some of your own things first will help you figure out the selling side of Ebay. You'll learn about taking photos, writing listings, answering customer questions, and shipping packages. The goal with selling a few things of your own first isn't to make a lot of money but to gain experience.

Only after you've become comfortable selling some of your own things should you venture out to find more items to resell. Again, just as you eased into using Ebay by buying a few items and then selling some of your own things, proceed with caution when you are at your first garage sales and thrift stores. You don't have to find 100 things to sell in one day. Take your time by buying a few things, getting them listing, shipping them out, gaining experience, and then using the money you make to buy some more items to resell. In the reselling business, we call this "Buying Your Education"!

These first steps into buying and selling on Ebay will not only help you gain experience, but you'll also start accumulating feedback, which is crucial to selling successfully on Ebay. A few negative feedbacks could quickly end your Ebay career, so proceed with caution. I have seen many new Ebay sellers have their accounts suspended by Ebay simply because they rushed into selling and made mistakes in their listing and shipping. As I tell people time and again, take it slow!

While there is no better way to learn how to sell on Ebay than actually going through the process yourself, it's also important to learn as much as you can through books, videos, and advice from other sellers. When I first started selling on Ebay, I sought out knowledge from every source I could find. I ordered several Ebay how-to books from Amazon (remember back when Amazon only sold books?!), I worked all of the tutorials and watched every video in Ebay's Seller Central section; and I lurked on the Ebay message boards. Today there are thousands of Ebay how-to videos on YouTube (mine included; the link to my channel is at the end of this book); and you can also join Facebook groups for Ebay sellers. There is also a large community of Ebay sellers on Instagram.

I encourage you to not only use this book to learn about Ebay, but to also seek out all of these other sources of information. Ebay is constantly growing and evolving, and the most successful sellers grow and evolve along with it. I've been selling on Ebay for over a decade now, but I still learn something new about it every day.

Remember that Ebay isn't your business but rather a tool you use in your business. You have to do things Ebay's way; and 99.9% of the time, Ebay sides with the buyer during any disputes. Ebay has also cracked down in recent years on sellers who consistently have customer issues. However, if you take the time to gather the necessary tools, go through the buying process yourself, and learn how to properly list and ship your items according to Ebay's specifications, you will avoid most problems.

CHAPTER 2

TIPS & TRICKS FOR CREATING GREAT EBAY LISTINGS

You've just come home from a day of thrifting and have bags full of great stuff you can't wait to get listed on Ebay. The best thing to do is jump right in, take a few pictures, and put everything online as fast as you can, right? WRONG! A lot goes into creating a great Ebay listing that will not only result in you getting the best price but also in a happy customer who leave you positive feedback.

Follow the steps below to create great listings that will result in fast sales and maximum profits!

Research: Before I list anything on Ebay, I first research it to see what the going price for it is or even if it actually selling. The way I do this is by doing a completed listing search. I simply type in a general description of my item in the search bar (for instance, "Pink Pyrex Bowl"); and I then narrow down the search fields, which appear on the left side of the screen. Included in those search fields is one for "Completed Listings". Selecting "Completed Listings" will show me what, if anything, an item has recently sold for.

If a completed listing search brings up several hundred listings, I will further narrow it down by selecting the "Sold" listings. Now instead of showing me every item that was listed in the past few months, regardless of whether it sold or not, selecting "Sold" will only show the listings that actually ended up a sale. You can then sort the results using several options, including most recently ended, distance, or price; I prefer to sort using the highest price so that I can see which items sold for the most money.

Often, I will find an item with a wide range of selling prices, and I then examine the results to see why some sold for a high price while others only sold for a few dollars. Often times it is because the seller had a low asking price, either starting an item at auction for only 99-cents or listing it at Fixed Price for just a few dollars. I base my price on the highest price an item went for, usually pricing it a bit lower than top dollar to ensure it sells faster.

Note that it's very important to base the selling price of the item you are listing on not only the comparable sales results but also on condition. While a brand-new book may bring in top dollar, a used one may only bring in a few bucks. Make sure that when you are looking at the completed listing results that you are basing the price of your item on the ones that are in similar condition to yours.

I also use the completed and sold search results to tell me if the item usually only sells with "free" shipping. As I will discuss later on in this book, shipping is never really "free" as someone, either the seller or the buyer, ultimately has to pay for the postage. However, some categories, such as clothing, are so crowded and competitive that building the cost of postage into the asking price in order to list the item with "free" shipping is often necessary to get the sale. Again, I will talk a lot more about shipping later in this book.

While I do most research in my office at my computer, when I am out and about, I sometimes look up items on my smart phone using Ebay's mobile app. That way I can quickly find if an item is worth me picking up or if I should pass on it. The downside to using Ebay Mobile for me is that I often run into problems finding an internet connection (especially when I am at an estate sale in the country). I've even had difficulty getting an internet connection inside of Goodwill stores. So, while it would be nice to be able to look up every item before I buy it, I often have to rely on instinct and wait until I get back to my office to do any research.

Remember that an item in only worth what someone will pay for it. Therefore, looking at the active Ebay listings isn't going to be much help as those results only show what sellers are currently ASKING for the item. The completed listings will show you what customers have actually PAID for it. This is often the biggest mistake new Ebay sellers make. I also hear this a lot from people selling their items at garage sales. "It's selling for $1000 on Ebay!" they'll claim; but they've usually only looked at the active listings, not the sold results.

Some categories, specifically clothing, require you to list the size of the item you are selling. While most clothing sizes are straightforward, sometimes I do need to research how various clothing brands size their garments. For instance, Chicos, which is a women's clothing company, has their own unique sizing chart that ranges from 000 (extra small) to 4.5 (extra-large). I also often have to research whether a piece of clothing is vintage (say, a pair of Levi's jeans) and how to spot counterfeit items (such as how to tell a real Coach purse from a fake).

I also pick up a number of products from overseas that aren't labeled in English; fortunately, Google is able to quickly translate most languages to English. I've found a number of German Bibles and hymnals over the years that I needed help translating; and I've also gotten pottery that was marked in a foreign language. I simply type in the book title or makers mark into the Google search bar following by "translate to English" in order to get a translation.

If, like me, you are dealing with vintage and collectible items, you may need to do further research on a piece in order to provide the most information about it as possible. For instance, I sell a lot of vintage flatware sets. These sell best when I am able to identify the pattern; so, I visit sites such as silvertableware.com and replacements.com to find the name, manufacturer and date of the sets I am selling.

Again, a simple Google search will bring up all kinds of resources for most objects you are selling. Nearly every collectible item has at least one dedicated website, often run by actual collectors that you can use to research everything from pottery to clothing. Don't just rely on Ebay to do your research; use the World Wide Web to learn as much as you can about the items you are selling. The more information you can provide, the more likely your item will sell fast and for top dollar!

Clean & Repair: When I come home from the thrift store or an estate sale, the first thing I do is lay everything I bought out on a table so that I can look it all over for damage. Even though I always inspect items before I buy them, it's not at all uncommon to end up finding ceramics with cracks or clothes with stains once I get them home.

If I find an item with damage, I decide whether or not it can be repaired. While I can easily tighten up a loose button, I can't repair a coffee mug with a giant chip in it. If an item can't be fixed, I either throw it away or donate it to Goodwill. The Goodwill stores in my area actually advertise that they will take all damaged goods as they recycle broken materials. They also sell bulk pallets of salvage fabric overseas. Before you donate damaged goods to your local thrift store, be sure to check their policy as some send unsellable items to the dump. If that is the case, see if you can recycle or reuse them on your own. For instance, we cut up damaged clothing and use the scraps for cleaning cloths.

After I've weeded out the damaged goods, I start cleaning the remaining items. First thing is to remove all price stickers and tags. For items where the price was written in marker, I use paint thinner or nail polish remover to wipe it off. Hand sanitizer can be used to get marker out of clothing tags. Sometimes marker print comes off easily, whereas other times I really have to scrub.

I wash all ceramics, carefully dust electronics, thoroughly search and clean out purses and bags, wipe off old books, and wash all clothing (unless it's leather or suede). While many sellers do not wash clothing, I prefer to as I'm not sure where the item has been before I purchased it at the thrift store. Therefore, I like to only handle clean clothing when I go to list the piece on Ebay.

Taking the time to clean your items will not only help them look better in photos, but customers who open their package to find clean items will be more likely to leave positive feedback. I take the "Golden Rule" approach to cleaning and repair of the items I sell on Ebay, making them look the way I would want them to if I were the customer!

Auction vs. Fixed Price: What makes Ebay such a unique selling platform are all of the different ways you can sell items. You can run auctions from three to 10 days; and you can also, for an added fee, include a "Buy It Now" price. Or you can list an item at fixed price for three to 30 days, or "good till canceled". Then there is the "Best Offer" option, which you can add to your listings. This allows you to review offers from customers and either accept, decline or negotiate. And finally, Ebay recently added the ability for sellers to send buyers an offer. With so many choices, no wonder new sellers have a hard time deciding how best to list their items!

The bottom line is that all Ebay listings, despite the length and added options, will either be auctions or fixed price. Think of the other options as add-on features, which I'll go over more in a bit. But first, how do you know whether or not you should start an item at auction or put it up as fixed price? The answer depends on the item itself.

If you have done your research and found that the item you are selling commands a steady price of, say, $50 on Ebay, then go ahead and list yours for $50 at fixed price. If you find your item is selling for a wide range of prices, you may want to price yours in the middle. So, if your item is selling from anywhere between $20 and $60, you may try pricing yours at fixed price for $40 to ensure a quick sale.

However, if you can't find any "sold" results for your item or if you see that the item typically brings in a lot of bidders at auction, you may want to try listing yours at auction, too. While you can run an Ebay auction from three to 10 days, I personally prefer running auctions for seven days. Seven days gives potential customers an entire week to find your item listing and decide if they want to bid.

As far as adding the "Buy It Now" option to auctions, I personally rarely do this as it costs extra; and I try to keep my Ebay fees as low as possible. If I have a good idea of how much an item will sell for, I just list it at fixed price rather than bother with the auction as, again, I'm only doing auctions for items I have no idea how to price. I don't want to add in a "Buy It Now" price in case the bidding price would actually end up higher.

If I think an item should realistically sell for $19.99, I'm not going to list it at auction for $9.99 with a $19.99 buy it now price as the item would likely end up only selling for $9.99. And if an item has the potential of selling for $50, I'm not going to start it at an auction of $9.99 with a buy it now of $19.99 as I am severely limiting my profit potential. In both of these cases, adding in the buy it now option would not only result in me selling my item for less, but I'd also have to pay additional listing fees.

While Ebay started off as an auction site, the landscape has changed a lot over the years. It's now very hard to get the price you want at auction as customers are becoming used to and now usually prefer to buy things at fixed price over bidding on them at auction.

I personally only do an auction if I have absolutely no idea what to price my item at, usually because I can't find another one like it online. However, I also occasionally use auctions on items that have been sitting around in my store for a while, as utilizing auctions is a great way to bring traffic to your other listings. However, I list the vast majority of my items at fixed price for 30 days.

Best Offer: When you list an item at fixed price on Ebay, you have the option of allowing buyers to send you offers via the "Best Offer" feature. It's easy to add this option to your listings; you just check the box under the price to enable customers to submit offers to you. You can choose to accept or decline offers automatically or you can choose to personally review each offer. For instance, if you have an item priced at $50, you can choose to automatically accept any offer of $40 or more; or you can choose to automatically decline any offers under $39.99. However, as I said, you can leave the settings open so that you can review every offer.

When you do get an offer, you have 48 hours to review it and reply. You can outright refuse the offer, which closes the communication between you and the buyer. If that buyer wants to send you another offer, they'll have to start the "Best Offer" process again. Some buyers like to send ridiculously low offers, such as offering $1 for a $50 item. These people obviously have no real interest in actually buying the item, so I do not engage with them; I simply decline their offer. If they are pesky and message me or submit another low offer, I will block them.

However, if you get an offer, you can choose to send a counteroffer; this is what most sellers do for reasonable offers from buyers they feel really do want an item. Let's go back to that $50 item. You have it listed at fixed price with the "Best Offer" option. A potential customer sends you an offer of $30. You can then counter, say with $40. If they buyer accepts, they will then be required by Ebay to complete the transaction at that price. Or they may want to continue to negotiate by submitting a counteroffer of $35; again, you can accept this or counteroffer again yourself, either for your original $40 offer or for one a couple of dollars less, say $38.

Sometimes, however, counteroffers are not accepted or completely ignored. While this can be frustrating, it's just a part of the unique Ebay selling platform. Don't get discouraged by customers who send low-ball offers or refuse your counteroffers; just move on and eventually the right buyer will come along.

Note that you want to carefully review all offers to make sure the offer doesn't include a change to the shipping price as well as the asking price. I've had buyers send me an offer that also stipulated I would give them free shipping. For instance, they'll offer me $5 plus free shipping for an item I had listed for $10 with the buyer paying shipping. Had I accepted those terms I would have essentially had to PAY to send them the item. So be very careful to understand the terms you are agreeing to when you accept a "Best Offer".

As far as adding the "Best Offer" option to my own listings, I only do this after an item has been listed for 30 days. If I list something for $50 and after 30 days it ends without selling, I will relist it but add in the "Best Offer" option. I don't do this the first time around as I want to try for the maximum selling price; and when you have the "Best Offer" option active, most customers are likely to try and negotiate.

I usually set "Best Offer" to automatically decline any offer that is less than 50% of my asking price. If I was willing to take half for an item, I would just list it for that. As for which offers I will accept, I look carefully at the item itself, what I originally paid for it, how long I've had it listed, and what I realistically think it should go for. I will generally accept offers of 25% or less of my asking price; if the offer is between 26-51% of my asking price, I will usually send a counter offer to try to get closer to the 25% mark.

I also only negotiate using the official Ebay "Best Offer" platform; I do NOT accept offers or make deals using the Ebay messaging system or with people who email me directly. It's very common for buyers to directly message sellers with offers or requests for free shipping; I generally just ignore these messages or reply telling them that I only negotiate on items that have the "Best Offer" option on them.

Don't let potential customers bully you into selling your items for less. Buyers who send direct messages asking for a discount usually do so because they know that the item is actually worth what you have listed it for and they are trying to snatch it away before another buyer comes along.

Pricing: While I do a completed listing search for every item I list on Ebay to try and determine a price, I do stick to a few key price points: $9.99, $24.99, $49.99, and $99.99. I choose these amounts for two reasons: One, these were the price points Ebay used to charge different fees for back when I first started selling; and while they no longer do this, it was this way for years and I've yet to break the habit. Two, customers have been trained to look for prices ending in 99-cents. After all, aren't you more willing to buy something that is priced at $24.99 as opposed to $26.45?

Sticking to these price points has worked well for me over the years. Of course, if I have done my research and found that an item is selling for a different amount, I will certainly price it accordingly. And I will also accept offers or run sales for lesser amounts. These numbers are my base prices, not always my final prices.

There are many sellers who will price items at $9.97 or $24.98 in hopes that their items will appear before $9.99 or $24.99 in Ebay searches. However, it's important to remember that Ebay shows items based on the total price including shipping. So, if your shipping is higher than the competition, your listing will still appear after others despite any difference in the price of the item itself.

For auctions, I generally won't start the bidding lower than $9.99. If you start your auction at 99-cents, do so only if you are using the auction to draw traffic to your other listings or if you are for sure that a bidding war will ensue. Otherwise, don't be upset when your item only sells for 99-cents. Ebay is flooded with 99-cent items, so be careful not to devalue your items by getting them lumped into the 99-cent listings that permeate the site.

In fact, you want to start ALL of your auctions at the MINIMUM price you will be happy accepting. If you want at least $20 for something, don't start the auction at $5, start it at $19.99. I see so many new sellers lose money by pricing their items too low, both at auction and fixed price. Not only do these sellers not make as much money, but the item itself gets devalued across the board. Again, do your research to find out what your item goes for on average and price yours accordingly.

Immediate Payment: One way to protect yourself from customers clicking to buy your item but then not paying is to require immediate payment. This can obviously only be done on fixed price items, not auctions; and it may not work if you are a seller that frequently sells multiple items in the same transaction as it prevents you from combining a customer's order. For instance, if you specialize in golf accessories, you may sell several items in one transaction to the same customer; and being able to send them an invoice with combined shipping is important.

Note that you can set up automatic shipping discounts for customers who buy multiple items, either giving them a percentage or dollar off discount, or automatically providing free shipping when they spend a certain amount of money. This works best if all of your items tend to be the same size and weight, for instance if you sell CD's or DVD's.

It's much easier to estimate shipping costs when all of your products weigh the same amount.

For example, you may set your shipping discounts to give customers free shipping when they buy three or more items. Or you may give them $1 off for every item they buy after the first one. So, if they buy three $5 items, they will pay $5 for the first, and then $4 each for the other two.

However, if you are like me and sell mostly unique, individual items, requiring immediate payment can save you the hassle of dealing with non-paying buyers. The option to require immediate payment is available in the payment section of all Ebay listings. I tend to be somewhat flexible on putting immediate payment on my listings by only using it for high price items. For small items under $25, I generally do not have immediate payment turned on as these are the items that are more likely to be purchased in multiples by the same customer. While one person may buy three $10 coffee mugs from me, it's rare one person will come along and purchase three $100 silverware sets at the same time.

Handling Fees: Ebay allows sellers the option to tack a handling fee on to all orders. It's up to the seller how much, if anything to charge; some sellers add 25-cents to each listing, while others add in several dollars. The reason to include a handling fee is to offset the cost of shipping materials such as boxes, tape, and packing paper; although some sellers try to charge enough in handling fees to profit on shipping.

Handling fees get added to the shipping cost of the item, so buyers don't necessarily see the added cost; however, savvy shoppers will notice if your shipping price is higher than another seller with the exact same item.

When I first started selling on Ebay in 2005, I had a 50-cent handling fee on all of my listings. However, I dropped that fee years ago. By researching prices and using calculated shipping (more about shipping coming up later in this book), I keep my costs low and don't need to pass on any extra fees to my customers.

To remain competitive, I recommend NOT tacking a handling fee on to your orders. Even a dollar more on top of the price of your product plus shipping can push the cost of your item too high in comparison to other sellers. Ebay is a huge marketplace with millions of sellers and buyers on the site every day. You have to do everything in your power to attract customers to your products, meaning you need to keep your selling and shipping prices as low as possible.

Selling online is all about volume; the more you sell the more money you make. Some sellers use handling fees to try and MAKE money; but this is a poor strategy. Not only will you lose potential customers because your shipping is too high, but you run the risk of buyers leaving you less than four stars in your feedback shipping rating.

If you buy low and sell high (i.e. buy items as cheap as possible so that you can mark them up for a decent profit) then you won't need to rely on handling fees to pad your wallet. And if you print your labels directly from Ebay, you will receive a shipping discount that will help offset the cost of packing materials. I'll talk more about shipping later on in this book.

Category: Before you even get to the pricing section of an Ebay listing, you'll need to fill out several other fields, the first being the category of the item you are selling. There are hundreds of Ebay categories and subcategories to choose from; and narrowing down which to list your item in can be overwhelming.

Many categories are obvious. If you are selling a cookbook, you will choose the "Books" category and then the "Cookbooks" subcategory. However, for items you are unsure of, type a general description of the item into the search field to see what turns up. Ebay will show you a list of available categories, the first one being the most commonly used. While the first option is usually the one you'll end up going with, be sure to look over the other choices to see if one is a better fit for your specific item.

You can also look at the categories similar items have sold in. Simply do a "sold" completed listing search and open a few of the highest priced sales to see which categories they were listed in and follow suit.

Ebay gives you the first category for free, but you can pay to have your item listing in a second category. Never once in all of my years selling on Ebay have I ever paid for a second category; and I recommend you don't, either. One category selection is all you need as it's not just the category but the title, photos, description, and shipping that help your item to be found when customers are using Ebay's search tool.

Listing Title: More important than the category you list your item in, however, is the listing title itself. The title of your Ebay listing is what search engines use when customers search on either Ebay or an internet search tool such as Google or Internet Explorer. A poorly worded title may not even get picked up in the search results, but a keyword-loaded title will bring in the maximum number of views, which in turn gives your item the best chance of actually selling.

When writing a title for your Ebay listing, it's important to remember that you don't need to write a perfectly structured sentence. Instead, you want to load up all of the available space with keywords that will not only be picked up in Ebay's search but also by Google and other internet search engines. Keywords are the key when writing your title, so fit in all the words you can, putting the most important words first.

For example, if you are selling a Ralph Lauren shirt, you don't want to simply put "Ralph Lauren Shirt" as your title. Rather, you want to load the space up with keywords by writing something like "Red Mens Polo RALPH LAUREN Dress Shirt LARGE Pony Logo Stretch". Note that the title doesn't read like a sentence but rather focuses on keywords that buyers are likely to type into the search engines.

I like to write my titles with each word capitalized. "Red Ralph Lauren Mens Shirt" looks a lot better and more professional than "red ralph lauren mens shirt" or even "Red Ralph Lauren mens shirt", doesn't it?

Don't waste space on silly words or phrases such as "L@@K" or "Open Now", which bring in zero traffic. Pull every single keyword you can think of including color, material, size, country of origin, and/or unique features from the item you are selling and cram those words into the title.

Just as you can pay to list your item in a second category, you can also pay extra to include a subtitle. Again, just as I never pay for a second category, I never pay for subtitles. Ebay offers plenty of space in the title section to load it up with keywords; don't spend money on a subtitle that most buyers won't even look at.

You'll also want to avoid punctuation in your titles. Notice how in the above example how I wrote "Mens" instead of "Men's"? Punctuation not only takes up valuable space that could be used for additional keywords, but punctuation can also interfere with search results. Another thing that can happen with punctuation is that it can mess up the entire word depending on what browser or computer the customer is using, making the words appear as a collection of characters (i.e. *!&#^) rather than letters.

When writing anything online, including your Ebay title, it's important to not type in all capital letters. Tying in all caps is the online equivalent of yelling, so you want to avoid it as it is very off-putting for the reader. Capitalizing the most important words helps the title stand out; putting all of the letters in capitals would make it distracting and even unreadable to some customers.

For example, "Red Mens Polo RALPH LAUREN Dress Shirt LARGE Pony Logo Stretch" has three words in all caps while the rest of the words only have their first letters capitalized. The most important words pop out at the buyer, drawing them into the listing. However, when the title is in all caps, i.e. "RED MENS POLO RALPH LAUREN DRESS SHIRT LARGE PONY LOGO STRETCH", it's hard for the eye to pick out any works as the type pretty much runs together, thus turning off potential customers.

Loading up the main title field with keywords, capitalizing the first letter of every word, avoiding punctuation, and capitalizing two or three main keywords all are quick and easy tricks that will go a long way towards selling your item fast and for top dollar!

Item Specifics: Ebay provides not only a space for writing your own listing description but also fields to fill in for item specifics. The listing specifics fields vary depending on what category you are listing in; clothing usually has a lot of details you can provide (brand, size, fabric, color), while other categories may only have a couple of choices.

It is important to fill in all of the item specific fields you can as these are used by customers to narrow down the search results. Buyers can choose clothing results by pattern, for example; so not selecting "striped" for the shirt you have listed means it may not come up in search. For very crowded categories such as clothing, the item specifics are what can make or break a sale as they are crucial to helping customers find your listings.

Filling in these fields correctly not only goes a long way towards describing the items you are selling but this information also protects you in case of customer complaints. Perhaps a customer says they thought the shirt they were buying was a size "large", not an "extra-large". However, if you put "extra-large" in the item specifics, that will prove to Ebay that you accurately described the product. However, you do need to provide the same specifics in the title and description field. If you have "extra-large" in the item specifics size field but "large" in the title and description field, the customer will be in the right to demand a return and refund.

While you want to fill in as many item specifics as you can, I also recommend you put those same details in the actual item description, too. While it's easy to assume customers will look at the item specific fields, some buyers skip over them and only look at the listing description. On the other hand, some customers may only look at the item specific fields. To cut down on potential buyer questions, include the information in both sections.

Item Description: In the item description field, you want to not only include everything you provided in the item specific fields, but you want to really try and "sell" your item by including something like "This stylish jacket will work on its own or layered with a tee-shirt!" or "This hard-to-find piece is a must for any collector!" There are hundreds of thousands of listings on Ebay at any one time, and you want to make sure your listing stands out from the competition.

There are all kinds of borders you can add to your listings, as well as fonts and colors you can use. However, I prefer to keep things simple by keeping the background white and the text black in a simple font. The only "dressing up" I do is to center the text, make it bold, and use a slightly larger font size. You have to remember that buyers are using all sorts of different browsers and devices to shop on Ebay, so you want to make things as uniform and simple as possible in order for your listings to appear clearly.

As I said, I like to center my item description lines with a space in between them. I "bold" the text and use size 14 Ariel font. I also only use black for the font color. And at the bottom of the listing, I put my term of service:

PAYMENT: Payment is due via PayPal within 4 days.

DAMAGES & RETURNS: Any damages must be reported to us within 30 days of receiving your package. A photo of the damage is required in order to qualify for a refund. If you want to return an item, you must contact us within 14 days of receiving your order. Refunds will be issued once we have the item back in the same condition in which we originally shipped it. Return postage is the responsibility of the customer. We cannot refund the original cost of postage.

SHIPPING INFORMATION FOR U.S. CUSTOMERS: We work hard to offer the lowest possible shipping price to our customers. We offer Media Mail for books and other media that qualify for this service; but please note that Media Mail can take a very long time to arrive. We ship via First Class for packages 16-ounces or less. We then offer Parcel Select and Priority Mail for packages weighing over 1 pound. We ship within two business days (i.e. weekday, not on weekends or holidays) after payment has cleared.

SHIPPING INFORMATION FOR INTERNATIONAL CUSTOMERS: We now ship all international orders via Ebay's Global Shipping program.

I see so many listings where sellers take up most of the space "threatening" potential buyers with statements like, "You must pay or else I will report you!" or "Don't bid unless you actually want the item!". While it can be tempting to "put your foot down", so to speak, these statements will turn customers away and can even invite trouble. While I do include a "Terms of Service" in my listings, it is at the very bottom of each listing and in a smaller font. I keep my actual listing verbiage upbeat and positive. After all, you wouldn't want a clerk "yelling" at you when you enter a brick-and-mortar store; so, treat potential Ebay customers with care.

Details: Some Ebay categories require much more than just stating what the item is and providing a general description. When I list a vintage book, I copy down all of the information on the title page (title, author, editor, publishing house, year), provide the number of pages, and measure the length and width of the book. When I sell vintage hymnals, I not only put the number of pages, but also the number of songs (sometimes hymnal will have 300 pages but contain 400 songs as some songs are so short that two to three can fit on the same page).

In fact, just as I do with books, simply copying what is on the outside of a box or on the bottom of an electronic is the best and fastest way to accurately describe items in more detail. Instead of listing a vintage clock radio simply by what brand it is, turn it over and copy whatever is on the bottom (country of manufacture, watts) into your listing. Even if the words make no sense to you (I honestly don't know what the number of Watts or Volts means!), a buyer who is specifically searching for the product you are selling will understand. And providing these details upfront will cut down on questions from potential customers as everything they need to know is already in the listing.

For clothing, you'll need to provide measurements. A size large shirt in one brand measures completely different in another. To measure shirts and jackets, I lay the garment on a flat surface. I then take three measurements, all in inches: pit-to-pit (tape measure drawn from under one armpit across to the other), sleeve (tape measure drawn from the shoulder seam to the cuff; if there is no should seam, I measure from the collar to the cuff, noting this in this listing); and body length (tape measure drawn from the top of the inside collar seam down to the hem).

For pants and skirts, I also lay the garment on a flat surface and measure the waist (tape measure drawn from one side of the waist to the other). I give an inseam measurement for pants (tape measure drawn from the crotch to the hem); for shirts, I give a length measurement (tape measure drawn from waist to hem).

In addition to providing the clothing measurements, I also explain HOW I took the measurements. Is this all a lot of extra work? Yes. But it serves two very important purposes. Number one is that it greatly reduces customer questions as I provide ALL information in the listing. And number two is that is significantly reduces the number of returns. In fact, it's very rare anyone returns a piece of clothing to me because it didn't fit; and if it didn't fit, it is the buyer who is to blame for not checking the measurements.

Details, details, details; it's all in the details. Taking the time to include everything single detail about the item you are selling into the listing will not only help you get top dollar but will also result in a happy customer. And happy customers leave positive feedback!

Relist vs. Sell Similar: When relisting an item, don't automatically choose the "Relist" option; a better choice is actually "Sell Similar". When you simply relist an item, it gets put back onto the Ebay site with its original item number, which says to Ebay that it is an item that has been on the site for a while. However, when you choose "Sell Similar", the item specifics will all remain the same, but the listing will get a new Ebay item number and be put into the Ebay search engine as a newly listed item.

With so many items for sale on Ebay, one way Ebay keeps listings fresh for buyers is to give priority to newly listed items. Selecting "Relist" will just get your item buried further down in the search results as Ebay will see it as something that has been on the site for a long time.

However, "Sell Similar" makes it a brand-new listing that will be put into the "Newly Listed" search.

The exception to choosing "Relist" over "Sell Similar" would be if the item that has ended had a lot of watchers and had gotten a lot of traffic. If that is the case, you may want to stick with "Relist" so that those buyers will still have it in their watch lists. If I have an item end after 30 days without any watchers, I will use the "Sell Similar" feature to relist it; however, if an item has at least one watcher but ends after 30 days without selling, I will use the "Relist" option so that the person who has been watching it will still have it in their "watch" list.

Whichever you choose – "Sell Similar" or "Relist" – it's a great time to give your listing another look to examine reasons why it hasn't sold. Your title may need to be reworked to add in more keywords. Perhaps you could redo some photos or add in better measurements. There may be more information you can include, such as filling in more item specific fields or adding more details into the description. Or you may consider adjusting the price or adding in a free shipping option. Just because an item ended its initial run without selling doesn't mean that there aren't things you can do to improve the listing so that it will sell the next time around!

Creating a New Listing: When I have a new item to list, instead of starting to list it from scratch, I simply open up an active listing and click on the "Sell a similar item" option in the top left corner. I then change the category (if needed), title, photos, item specifics, description field, and shipping weight; however, all of my other settings, such as my shipping and return policies, remain in place.

Creating a new listing off of an active one makes the listing process go a lot faster as I don't have to reset my policies and requirements. I often list a number of like items in a row, such as coffee mugs, Bibles or clothing. This allows me to keep a lot of the information that is in the description field the same; I just change the specifics of each pieces. For instance, if I am listing coffee mugs that are all the same brand and size but have different patterns, the only changes in the new listing I will need to make are changing the pattern in the title, item specifics, and description field, as well as adding in the new photos. Everything else such as the brand, measurements, and materials remain the same.

If you do use this "Sell a similar item" trick, just make sure to change ALL of the relevant information such as the category, title, item specifics, item description, and package weight. I have been careless at times and overlooked writing a new title in – oops! I've also accidently left the "free shipping" option checked for an item I actually expected the customer to pay shipping on. While using the "Sell a similar item" feature is fast and easy, it can also make you lazy; so be sure to look over your listing carefully after it goes live to make sure all of the information and settings are correct.

Full Disclosure: It's important to be completely honest in your Ebay listings. Customers are taking you at your word that an item is as you state; if they find a flaw or error that you didn't disclose, it will come back to you in the form of an unhappy buyer, a return, and/or negative feedback.

Since most items sold on Ebay are secondhand, it is vital that you look over the pieces you are selling very carefully to find any flaws. Even a small mark that you doubt anyone else will see should be disclosed. Don't list an item as "MINT" when it in fact was found on the floor of a thrift store. "MINT" means that the item just rolled off the assembly line. I usually understate the condition of my items. If I have something in excellent condition, I list it as great. If it is great, I list it as good.

If I buy an item at an estate sale and know for sure that the original owner was a non-smoker, I will state, "From a clean, smoke-free home!" in the listing. I wash all ceramics, and I also wash clothes in non-scented detergent because a lot of people are sensitive to fragrances. I've actually had a number of customers over the years message me to specifically request that I do not put a dryer sheet in their package, which is a trick some sellers use to make clothing appear fresher. I do everything I can to make sure that items are as clean as possible so that they not only show up nicely in photos but also when they arrive to the customer.

The best piece of advice I ever got when I started selling on Ebay was to "under promise and over deliver". I try to understate the condition of items a bit so that buyers don't have unrealistic expectations. Often, I receive positive feedback that reads, "Better than expected" or "In much better condition than I was expecting".

CHAPTER 3

TIPS & TRICKS FOR TAKING QUALITY EBAY PHOTOS

While a great tile and description are extremely important when selling on Ebay, neither are enough to ensure a sale. Just as important (and in some cases even more so) are your product photos. Great pictures not only attract customers to your listings, but accurate photos help protect you as buyers know exactly what they are purchasing.

You don't have to be an expert photographer or have the most expensive equipment to take great Ebay photos. The following tips and tricks will help you to quickly and easily take pictures that will result in Ebay sales.

Item Pictures: Ebay allows sellers to add up to 12 photos per listing, so you should take full advantage of that and provide as many pictures as possible of the items you are selling. Take photos from every angle, including from the top and from the bottom. You want to give your customers the feeling that they would have if they were in a brick-and-mortar store handling an item. You likely don't purchase something by only glancing at it briefly on the shelf, so you will sell more on Ebay if you give your customers pictures of your items from every angle.

If you are selling a coffee mug, for instance, take pictures of the front, back, both sides, bottom, and of the inside. For clothes, take full-length shots of the front and back as well as up close pictures of hems, cuffs, pockets, and the label. If your item is battery-powered, take a photo of the open battery compartment to show that there isn't any erosion. When I list vintage books, I take photos of the front and back cover, the spine, the first couple of title pages, and two to three photos of the text pages.

You want the item you are selling to be front and center in all pictures, so take the time to edit your photos in order to eliminate as much white space as possible. Most computers come with easy-to-use built-in photo editing software; I use a PC and have Picasa, which came with my system and is powered by Google.

I take pictures with both a point-and-shoot digital camera as well as my iPhone. I make sure to take up-close photos of any condition issues such as minor wear or damage. I disclose any faults in the listing, and I also direct buyers to look closely at the photos provided so the know exactly what they are buying. It's rare to find secondhand items that don't have even a tiny bit of wear and tear; but by disclosing all issues and providing photos, you will not only have a better chance of the item selling, but you will also protect yourself from a customer complaining they received something that wasn't as described.

I often use my digital camera to take the main product photos and then use my iPhone to take up-close pictures of details such as maker's marks on ceramics, clothing labels, and inscriptions, as well as any condition issues. The cameras on most of today's smart phones take pictures that are just as good, and sometimes even better, than actual cameras; and my iPhone in particular is much better at capturing up-close details than my regular camera is.

After taking my pictures, I upload them to my computer and edit them in Picasa. Ebay prefers that photos be no smaller than 900x900 in dimension, so I crop out as much space around the item as possible while staying in those specifications. I have a dedicated folder on my

PC where I put all photos, which I delete after each batch has been listed onto Ebay.

When I am creating a new listing, I simply upload the photos from my computer to Ebay. Once on Ebay, I can then rearrange them to make sure certain photos are shown first. I arrange them to be viewed just as the person would be looking at the item in an actual store, examining the outside first before checking out the inside and any small details.

You want the main item photo, the one that will appear as the thumbnail in the Ebay search, to be the photos that show your entire item. For instance, if you are selling a coffee mug, you want the front of the mug to be the main picture, not the bottom. Make sure all photos are upright, not sideways or upside down; and do not upload blurry photos. I can't tell you how many bad item photos I see on Ebay; and poor-quality pictures can make it next to impossible for an item to sell. It's better to retake photos than upload poor ones.

Lighting: You don't need a fancy photography set-up to take Ebay photos, just a space with a lot of light. Good lighting is essential to take clear photos and to capture color and detail.

If your home or work space is dark, you can easily brighten things up with lamps. If you are frequently listing a lot of items online, you may want to invest in some professional lighting, although I myself never found this necessary. Even taking your items outside to photograph can help you get better light than you may have indoors.

A light box is a tool that sellers of small items such as jewelry like to use. Portable light boxes can be purchased for around $50 online, although there are all sorts of YouTube tutorials on how to make your own using cardboard boxes and lights. I myself own a light box, but I rarely get it out for photos. I find that these sorts of extra selling tools work best if you can leave them up permanently. Because I have to get mine out and then put it away every time I want to use it, I find myself not bothering with it.

I take my photos in a room with lots of windows that provide great natural lighting. I also turn on the lights to add more brightness. I want to make sure to capture the true color and texture of the items I am selling. Rarely do I use my camera flash as this often distorts the actual color of the product, making it appear lighter than it actually is.

Backdrops: I see so many Ebay sellers who take pictures of items on their dirty carpet or with their messy kitchen in the background. I have even seen pictures of packaged food products taken on the floor!

Taking pictures against a white background will work for most items, whether it is a white wall, a sheet or a table. I have a very simple set up of white poster boards for my photos. I set one on a table and the other against a wall to form a slight angle. I buy the boards at the dollar store for $1 each; and I also have a set in black for light-colored items that don't show up against a white background.

For larger items, it's easy to take pictures against a white wall. If you don't have a white wall, draping a white sheet from the ceiling can provide a nice backdrop. I have a blank white wall in my office with a single nail that I hang clothes from to take photos. You want to make sure that whatever backdrop you use is clean and pattern-free so that nothing takes away from the item itself.

Whatever you use as your backdrop, just make sure that the item you are selling is the only item in the picture. I can't tell you how many photos I see where other things and even people and pets are in the photos. Make sure to edit your hands/fingers out of pictures. I occasionally need to hold down a book page in order to get a photo, but I always edit my hand out. Unless you are a hand model, no one wants to see your chipped nails and cracked cuticles. Yuck!

Stock Photos: If you are selling an item with a bar code that is in Ebay's catalog, a stock photo will often pop up that you can use as the main picture in your listing. And while many sellers use these photos, I personally do not like them, preferring instead to use my own pictures. Sometimes I do use Ebay's provided stock photo, but not as the main picture; I keep it in the listing and have it at the end of my photo lineup.

Stock photos indicate the item is brand new; and even if you have a new, unused item to sell, you likely picked it up secondhand. So, there may be differences in the box you have over the stock photo, including slight damage. And unless an item is brand new and in Ebay's catalog with the photo they provide or you've obtained permission from the manufacturer, wholesale or liquidation company that the item came from, it's against policy to use that picture.

Again, it is illegal to use a company's stock photo without their permission. If you are purchasing items via wholesale or liquidation and those companies provide you with stock photos, you'll still need permission to use those pictures on Ebay. Do not go directly to a company's website and copy their pictures for your Ebay listing; not only will that get you into trouble with Ebay, but it could also result in legal action from the business whose photos you stole.

Even if the item I am selling matches the approved stock pictures exactly, I still take my own photos as I personally feel it best represents my specific product. While customers turn to Amazon to buy brand new items, they often come to Ebay looking for gently used products or extreme deals. So, while it's reasonable to expect an Amazon listing with an available quantity of one hundred products to use stock photos, on Ebay most people are just selling one single version. And by providing photos of the exact item you are selling you assure customers that what they see in the picture is exactly what they are getting.

While you will likely see other sellers using stock photos on Ebay, please remember that just because some people are getting away with it doesn't mean you should, too. Do you really want to risk losing your Ebay account because you didn't want to take a few pictures? I know I don't!

CHAPTER 4

TIPS & TRICKS TO EASILY PROMOTE YOUR EBAY LISTINGS

When I first started selling online, Ebay and Amazon were the only two ecommerce retailers. Customers who shopped online only had the two sites to choose from, so there was no need for sellers to seek out buyers. However, nowadays it's often not enough to simply list an item on Ebay for it to sell; you now have to do some promotion and marketing to drive sales.

Fortunately, social media provides lots of free and easy ways to promote your Ebay listings. By adding in some or all of the following methods of marketing, you'll see your Ebay traffic and sales increase. In some cases, you may need to spend a little bit of money (such as if you decide to set up a website and/or have enclosures printed up); but even then, the costs are still relatively low compared the huge differences they can make for your sales.

Blog/Website: If Ebay is your part-time or full-time business, it may be worth it to you to set up a blog or even a full-fledged website to further connect with customers. If you are going to have a site, however, be sure to commit to maintaining it. Nothing is worse than going to someone's blog and seeing that they haven't updated it in months.

However, if you are only selling on Ebay occasionally or just for a bit of extra money, then you really don't need to burden yourself with the work of maintaining a site. Ask yourself the following questions:

- Do you plan to write lengthy articles discussing the items you sell?

- Are you looking to use your site not just as a sales channel but also as a teaching tool?

- Would you like to sell products directly from your website outside of Ebay; or are you selling your items on other online sites (Amazon, Etsy) and/or at brick-and-mortar retail locations (your own shop or at an antique mall)?

- Would you like to explore affiliate advertising and/or sell advertising for your site to earn extra money?

If you answered "yes" to any of the above questions, then you may want to consider starting a site. However, you'll then need to decide whether to go with a free blogging platform or a paid website. If you decide to go the paid route, you can invest in a sophisticated system or choose a simple low-cost one. Yes, there are lots of decisions to make!

In addition to selling on Ebay, I also have a blog at AnnEckhart.com. I use my blog to promote my books and YouTube videos, many of which are devoted to teaching people how to make money on Ebay.

Before I started my current blog, I had dabbled in blogging a few different times on Blogger, which is Google's blog platform. I actually had a blog dedicated solely to Ebay. However, when I started AnnEckhart.com, I closed that blog and moved all content to my new website.

The difference between that Ebay blog and my current blog is that my Ebay blog was just a blog, whereas my AnnEckhart.com blog is technically a website that hosts my blog. So, I now have a blog ON a website.

Huh? A blog ON a website? Confused? Don't worry, I was, and still am sometimes, confused! Even today, I struggle with whether to call AnnEckhart.com a blog or a website. In the beginning, I called it a website, but these days I call it a blog, even though it is actually a website, mainly because the term "blog" is more popular in the social media world. Oy!

To put it simply, a blog that is on a free site such as Blogger or WordPress is just a blog. However, a website is a site that you own that utilizes blogging software. AnnEckhart.com is my website, and on my website, I use WordPress blogging software.

When you have a blog on a free site, it is actually not yours but instead belongs to the company behind the site you are using. It could be shut down at any time, and you would then lose all of your content. And while Blogger and WordPress have been around for years and show no signs of going anywhere, the risks are still there that you could eventually lose all of your content.

When I had my Ebay blog on Blogger, I didn't put anything important on it; I just posted about new listings and had the links to my social networking sites. I rarely even promoted the blog; I just maintained it so that if anyone happened to stumble across it, they would hopefully click through to my Ebay store.

However, my blog is actually a business for me as I earn income through affiliate advertising. I also load it with a lot of original content. If it were on a free blogging site, all of that information could be lost in a moment's notice. However, as long as I keep paying my website maintenance fees, my content is safe.

So, if you are just looking for another way to drive traffic to your Ebay listings, stick with creating a simple free blog that has links to your Ebay store and your other social networking sites. Try to update it a couple of times a week with a brief description of new listings or any sales you are running. Pictures are essential, too.

Both Blogger and WordPress offer free blogging platforms. Note, however, that Blogger is owned by Google; therefore, you can apply for a Google AdSense account and place ads on your blog. So not only will you be helping drive traffic to your Ebay listings in order to increase sales, you'll also be able to earn advertising revenue. Note that while I utilize WordPress blogging software on my website and have affiliate advertising on it, the FREE WordPress blog does not allow many forms of advertising. So, if you would like a free blog that allows ads, go with Blogger.

However, if you do decide to go with a paid website, do your research as there are a lot out there to choose from. I went with a large company (Bluehost.com) because I wanted my blog to be the centerpiece of my brand and because I wanted to utilize several forms of affiliate advertising on it. If your main business is selling on Ebay, you want your Ebay Store to be your brand with your blog/website acting as an additional tool to drive traffic to your listings. There a lot of low-cost website options out there. For instance, you can not only register for website URL's on GoDaddy.com, but they also offer website hosting.

For me, my blog is an actual business, a company that I earn an income from. While I do share Ebay information on my site, I also share recipes, reviews, and sponsored content. In addition to writing books like this one about Ebay, I also make YouTube videos about how I make money on Ebay. I share my books and videos on my blog, so all three (blog, YouTube, books) work together to promote each other.

So, which should you choose? A free blog or a website? Or no site at all? That is a decision only you can make. Having a blog or website for your Ebay business is NOT a requirement. In fact, it may actually be more work than is worth it for you. And as I will talk about later in this chapter, you may find that a Facebook page can just as easily act as your "website".

However, if you do decide to set up an Ebay blog or website, it doesn't have to be complicated. Think of it as the "home" page for your business where you provide the link to your Ebay store as well as the links to all of your other social networking sites (Facebook, Twitter, Pinterest, etc., which I'll discuss further in this chapter).

If you sell on other websites in addition to Ebay, a blog/website is a great place to provide the links to those places (Amazon, Etsy, flea markets, and/or antique malls). In addition to posting about new inventory and sales, you can include photos and talk about what is going on behind-the-scenes with your business. Having a site gives people a more personal look as to who you are and also confirms that fact that you are running a legitimate business, both of which can go a long way towards building up trust and reassuring people that they can buy from you with confidence.

Note that in addition to posting updates on your blog that you'll need to maintain it. If you allow visitors to leave comments on your posts, you'll want to make sure to respond to them. You also want to make sure all links are active and up-to-date so that people don't click through and get an error.

If you are selling a significant number of items on Ebay and plan to continue with it as your main business, you may want to register for a domain name, i.e. a personal website address that matches your Ebay Store name. For years, I maintained a URL of my Ebay Store name that sent people directly to my Ebay Store. Having a URL gives you an easy web address to share with customers that is shorter and easier to remember than the long store URL you would otherwise have to promote (i.e. http://stores.ebay.com/yourebaystorename). You can purchase domain names on a website like GoDaddy.com.

You'll also have to decide where you want the URL to direct. Do you want people to go to your blog FIRST, or do you want them to always go to your Ebay Store? Remember, you should be using a blog/website as a *compliment* to your Ebay Store, not as a replacement. If you decide to go with a free blog on a site like Blogger, you may want to choose a URL that sends people directly to your Ebay Store (i.e.

www.MyStore.com) and keep the URL you get from Blogger as is. Or choose another URL such as www.MyEbayStoreBlog.com.

My advice is that you have a personalized URL address that points to your Ebay store as getting Ebay sales should always be your first priority. Your site should work to direct traffic to your Ebay listings, not to intercept them.

Ebay Profile: Ebay allows you to provide a bit of information about yourself, which can help you connect with customers. What used to be a full-fledged "About Me" page has recently been downgraded to a simple paragraph space that customers see when they click on your seller name.

This space is available for you to edit when you are logged in; simply click on your screen name and your "Ebay Profile" page will appear as it looks to buyers but with the ability for you to edit the content. There are a limited number of characters available, so keep it short and simple. In my profile, I introduce myself, state that I have been selling on Ebay since 2005, and let buyers know that I specialize in vintage items, collectibles and clothing.

This profile page also allows you to upload a logo and a banner, as well as to add in collections and reviews. In addition to my store logo, I also include a picture of my dad and me so that buyers can see we are actual people selling the items in our store.

It's important to spend a few moments customizing your Ebay profile section. Connecting with customers on a personal level is a great way to encourage sales as it promotes a sense of familiarity between you and buyers. It also helps customers feel safe ordering from you as they feel as if they know you a bit.

Enclosures: When I first started selling on Ebay in 2005, I was adamant that I wasn't going to include a packing slip. After all, why should I spend more money on ink and paper for something that most customers would likely just throw away?

Fortunately, more experienced Ebay sellers counseled me on the importance of including a packing slip with all orders. After all, I expect a packing slip in MY packages when I place an order online. I am always put off when I open a box to only find the item I ordered inside but no packing slip. "Do on To Others" definitely holds true when it comes to putting packing slips into your Ebay packages! Now I can't imagine NOT including a packing slip inside of all of my outgoing orders, and I encourage all sellers to include them.

Ebay makes including a packing slip incredibly easy. After you print a shipping label, a screen comes up with the option to "Print a Packing Slip". Simply print it out, fold it up, and put it inside the box or envelope the item is being shipped out in.

I also like to include promotional enclosures in my packages that promote my Ebay store. I order standard-size postcards from VistaPrint with my store logo on them. On the card, I thank the customer for their order, provide them with the URL to my Ebay store, let them know I am on Facebook and Twitter, and give them a dedicated email address to send any questions or comments they may have.

Mailing List: When I sold new gift items, I tended to get a lot of repeat customers. I developed my own email mailing list by using the PayPal email address that I had access to once someone paid me. I simply copied and pasted email addresses into a Word document, and then put them in to the Blind Carbon Copy section of my email program when I wanted to send out a message.

When someone buys an item from you, you are able to email them once. HOWEVER, if they ask you to remove them from your mailing list, you must comply. For a time, I used the email newsletter service Constant Contact, which had an "unsubscribe" feature that people could easily use. Not everyone takes kindly to getting emails, so be prepared for some people to be angry if you email them a newsletter or sale notice.

I would only recommend developing a list like this through a service such as Constant Contact as trying to maintain it on your own is difficult. Since there is a cost involved, I would also only recommend an email program to large sellers who sell a lot of the same items and anticipate a number of repeat customers. I dropped my email list when I got out of the gift business, as nowadays most of my sales are to one-time buyers.

Facebook: If you plan to be selling a lot of items on Ebay, it is worth your time to set up a Facebook page to promote your listings. Some sellers choose to make their personal page their business page; but if you are already actively participating on Facebook by using your personal page to communicate with your friends and family, I recommend that you set up a separate business page. A personal page is one where people add you as a friend, while a business page is one people must "like".

I prefer the business page format for promoting Ebay listings because it keeps your personal life and business separate. There is a limit to how many friends you can add to a personal page, but you can grow an unlimited number of business "fans" on a business page. However, in order to start a business page, you do need to first have a personal page.

To set up a Facebook business page, simply visit facebook.com/about/pages. You'll need to log into your personal Facebook account first, and then the system will walk you through the steps needed to create your business page. It is FREE and easy to set up.

The first decision you'll need to make is to name your page. My Facebook business page is simply "Ann Eckhart"; but years ago, before I started that site, I did have a page that was the same name as my Ebay Store. And if you are starting the Facebook page specifically for your Ebay business, then you'll want to make the names match.

In fact, as you go forward with creating more social media accounts related to your Ebay business, you'll want to make sure they all have the same name. So now is the time to evaluate your Facebook user name to make sure it matches your Ebay store and that it is a good name overall. For instance, if you've been using the Ebay user name "i_luv_cats", you may want to change it to something more professional.

To change your Ebay username, simply go to **My eBay** and then **Account**. Click **Personal Information** on the left side of the page. Then click **Edit** to the right of the information you want to change.

To change the name of your Ebay Store, simply go to **My eBay, Account,** and then **Subscriptions**. On the **Manage My Store: Summary** page, scroll to the **Set Up, Sell and Track** section; and click the **Design Your Store** link. In the **Display Settings** section, click the **Change** link and make your edits.

Once you've gotten your Ebay username and Ebay Store name's straight, you can proceed with naming your Facebook page the same.

There are all kinds of things you can personalize on your Facebook page. You can add a profile picture and a banner. I have my logo as my profile picture; and I had a custom banner made on **Fiverr.com**. Whatever photos or graphics you choose, remember that this is your BUSINESS page, so keep it professional.

You'll also want to fill out the extensive **About** section in order to provide people with information about your page and business. However, since this is your BUSINESS page and separate from your personal page, you'll want to be careful with how much information you provide. While you may share your cell phone number on your personal page, unless you have a brick-and-mortar location that you actually want people to call, you'll want to leave that section blank on your business page.

You'll first need to choose the **Category** for your page; as an Ebay seller, there are several you can choose from such as "Companies & Organizations", "Local Businesses", or "Websites & Blogs". Any of the three would be fine for your Ebay page; it's really up to you which you prefer. You'll need to select a sub-category, too. And don't worry about being locked into your selections; you can easily change them at any time.

In addition to your **Name** (the name of your page, i.e. your Ebay business name), you can edit your Facebook URL so that it ends in that name.

The **About** section has fields for both a **Short Description** and a **Long Description**. I have my tagline in the Short section and a much more detailed account of what I do in the Long section.

Since you provided information about you and your business in the Short and Long Description sections, use the **General Information** field to share the links to your other social media sites. You'll want to put the address to your Ebay Store in the main Website field (remember, your main goal is to drive traffic to your Ebay listings), but add any other links you may have (blog/website, Twitter, Pinterest, Instagram, etc.) to the General Information section so that users can easily connect with you on all of your social media platforms.

One great feature you can add to your Facebook page is a **Shop Now** tab that will take users directly to your Ebay Store. Simply click on **More** at the top of the page and select **Manage Tabs** to add a **Call to Action – Shop Now** button. Link it to your Ebay Store to create an easy way to your Facebook fans to shop your Ebay listings.

Finally, at the top of the page, click on **Settings** to determine how users can interact with you. I have very strict privacy settings for my page. I don't allow people to message me or post on my wall. When I had these two features turned off, I was inundated with messages and posts. However, if having messages from people is okay with you, then by all means leave those options open. You can always change them later on.

Once you have your page set up, it's time to start building your audience by getting people to "Like" your page. You'll be able to invite the friends and family on your personal page to "Like" your new business page. If you are a part of Ebay groups, you can also post about your new page there and hope that fellow Ebayers will give you some support.

In order to bring customers (past, present or potential) to your Facebook page, include the link to your page on any package enclosures. I have business card sized "thank you" notes that go into every order printed with the direct link to my Ebay store. When I had a Facebook business page dedicated to Ebay, I also included that URL. Now that everything I do runs through See Ann Save, I have a separate card with the link to my blog and all of my social media pages.

So, you've set up a Facebook page for your business and have started getting people to "Like" it. Now what? Providing useful content on your page will be key to keeping it up to date and to attracting new followers.

When I had a Facebook page for my Ebay business, I would share my new listings to it. Ebay makes this incredibly easy to do. In the upper right-hand corner of all active Ebay listings are "share" buttons for Facebook, Twitter, Pinterest, and Email. Simply click on the Facebook icon, change the page you want to post to (it will show you your personal page and business page, so be sure to select your business page), type in something like "Just Listed!" or "On Sale!", and then hit "Share". In only a few seconds, many of the people who have "Liked" your page will now have your listing on their Facebook feed!

In addition to sharing listings, it's also a good idea to engage your Facebook fans by posting status updates about what is going on with your business, such as if you are getting in new inventory. You want to keep your business page postings POSITIVE; stay away from religious, political or other controversial topics. Remember, your goal with Ebay is to MAKE money, and you can't do that by offending people. Save the personal commentary for your personal Facebook page.

Posting pictures of your office, new inventory, or even a shot of orders ready to ship out are all fun ways to keep your audience interested. And sharing unique content is vital to ensure people actually SEE your posts.

Facebook is making it increasingly difficult for people to see all content on their feeds as Facebook wants page owners to purchase advertising. You may have noticed a little "Boost" link under your posts. "Boosting" a post means that you have to PAY for Facebook to show it to people. Pricing for this starts at $5; the more you pay, the more people Facebook will show your post to.

While this is incredibly frustrating, resist the urge to boost all of your posts. While it can be advantageous to spend $5 here and there to ensure a post gets seen, don't let yourself become consumed if every post doesn't reach a wide audience. It is likely that the links you share of your listings won't be shown to as many people as photos you post directly to your page (i.e. unique content).

I share the link to every blog post I write to my Facebook page, but it's the pictures I share directly to the page that get the most views and the most "Likes". Use this to your advantage by trying to post a new photo at least a few times a week in order to create engagement from your Facebook followers.

As I mentioned earlier, you may decide that a Facebook page can act as your blog or website rather than setting up a separate site. Many Ebay sellers do not have a blog or website, rather using Facebook as their homepage. So, unless you have the time to devote to maintaining a separate website, consider just using Facebook along with other social networking to promote your Ebay business. I recommend you do Facebook FIRST as you can always add a blog/website later on.

Facebook is just the first in a long list of social media sites you can create in conjunction with your Ebay business. Master your Facebook page first before moving on to the next social media account: Twitter!

Twitter: If you don't already have a Twitter account, you can create one for FREE at Twitter.com. If you do have an account that you are active on, consider creating a new one just for your Ebay business. As with Facebook, you want to keep your personal and business lives separate on Twitter. Make sure your Twitter handle is the same as your Ebay username, Ebay Store name, and Facebook business page name.

Twitter allows users to share posts of 140 characters or less. And just like Facebook, Twitter is a fast, easy and free way to promote your listings. As with sharing your listings to Facebook, Ebay makes is easy to share your listings to Twitter using the share button located in all active Ebay listings (in the upper right-hand corner).

To share a listing via Twitter, first you will want to copy the title of your listing to your clipboard (simply highlight and select "copy"). Ebay and Twitter often have a generic "check out what I found on Ebay" title already in place when you click on the Twitter share button, so you will want to replace that with your keyword-loaded title. Simply delete the text in the Tweet that you want to replace and paste in your title.

Adding in hashtags is another easy way to make sure your Tweet gets seen by potential customers. A hashtag is a pound (#) sign followed by a keyword, and it is what experienced Twitter users enter into the search field to seek out relevant Tweets. As an example, let's say you Ebay listing title is "Red Mens Polo RALPH LAUREN Dress Shirt LARGE Pony Logo Stretch". Put that into a new Twitter "tweet", followed by the link to the listing. And after the link, add in hashtags such as #RalphLauren #Polo #MensClothing.

Note that due to Twitter's restriction of 140 characters, you may need to cut down your listing title in order for it, the Ebay link and your hash tags to all fit. In the above example, you could easily drop the last three words (Pony Logo Stretch) from Twitter to make room. You want to keep the most relevant keywords, which in that case are "Red Mens Polo RALPH LAUREN Dress Shirt", followed by the link to the listing.

Just as you share your Facebook page with customers via a blog/website and/or package enclosures (as I've said, I include business card size "thank you" notes in all of my Ebay packages with my Ebay store link as well as all of my social media URL's), you'll also want to share your Twitter handle with them in the hopes they will follow you on Twitter, too. And to find even more followers, you'll want to actively engage with other Twitter users.

Some Twitter users follow everyone who follows them; and this can certainly be a way to build up your followers. You can also "network" with other folks on Twitter by replying to, retweeting, or favoring tweets. As I mentioned when setting up your Facebook page, you can add all of your social media links, including your Twitter URL, in the "About" section; so hopefully some of your Facebook fans will follow you to Twitter. To encourage this, about once a week post your Twitter link directly to your Facebook page to make it easy for people to click through and "follow" you.

What you'll want to gain from Twitter is people clicking through to your Ebay listing links and either purchasing that item or finding something else to buy from you. You will also likely see that some people "favor" your Tweets by clicking on the little star icon under each message. It's always nice when someone retweets one of your Tweets, too, so that it gets shared with their followers.

Note that just as people can message you on Facebook (unless you change the privacy settings to block them) you can also send and receive messages on Twitter. And finally, you can create "Lists" on Twitter to group people you follow together (such as "customers", "Ebay sellers", "celebrities", "news", etc.).

Pinterest: Pinterest started out as a way for people, mainly women, to "pin" craft ideas and recipes to virtual boards. However, Pinterest is quickly becoming a tool for businesses to get the word out about their products and to develop brand loyalty. Pinterest offers Ebay sellers another fast and free way to promote their listings in the hopes that people will click through and purchase products.

As with Facebook and Twitter, Ebay provides a Pinterest "share" button in all active listings (in the upper right-hand corner). I have a "For Sale on Ebay" board on Pinterest that I "pin" my listings to. Not only can my Pinterest followers then see my new listings, but they can share the pin with THEIR Pinterest followers by pinning it to their own boards.

You will find lots of other Ebay sellers on Pinterest, many of whom have created Ebay group boards that you may be invited to post to. Networking with fellow Ebay sellers on Pinterest is another great way to promote your listings while getting to know other Ebayers such as yourself. Re-pinning THEIR pins is a nice gesture and a great way to network.

One concern many Ebay sellers have is that once items sell, the "pin" is no longer relevant. Should you delete old pins of items that have sold? While you certainly can take the time to do this, you don't have to. In fact, it may be beneficial for you to leave the pin active. Why? Well, let's say someone sees a pin of a collectible you have for sale. When they click through, they find that the item has sold. However, they are now connected with you on Ebay and may click on the link to visit your Ebay store or to see your current listings. While they may be annoyed that the item they wanted is no longer available, they also might find something else to buy from you.

Just as you should be doing with your Facebook and Twitter links, be sure to share your Pinterest page with customers by including the link on your blog/website (if you have one), and in the General Information section of your Facebook page. You can also provide the URL to your Pinterest account in any package enclosures. Be sure to periodically share your Pinterest link on both Facebook and Twitter in order to attract new followers.

You may be noticing by now that a big part of social networking is to have all of your sites working together. Include all of your social media links on your blog/website and in package enclosures. Post your Twitter and Pinterest links to Facebook; share your Facebook and Pinterest links on Twitter. The more you can get your Ebay links out there, the easier it will be for customers to find you and for you to make more sales and make more money!

Instagram: Like Facebook, Twitter, and Pinterest, Instagram is easy and FREE to use! While Ebay doesn't yet provide a "share" button for Instagram, it is still a useful tool for promoting your listings. You can currently only add photos to your Instagram through their apps, so note that you will need to have a phone or tablet in order to use the site.

In addition to helping to drive traffic to your Ebay store, Instagram is also great for connecting with customers on a personal level by sharing photos that may not always relate directly to your business. However, as with anything you share on your business accounts, be sure to keep Instagram pictures non-controversial and lighthearted (i.e. avoid politics and religion!). Take photos of your office or of all the packages you are shipping out. Include pictures of your pets and even what you are having for lunch. Make it your goal to post at least one photo to Instagram every day.

Hashtags are a big part of getting your content on Instagram found. I like to include three to five hashtags with every photo I share. When I post a photo related to Ebay, I use hashtags such as "Ebay", "Ebayer", "Reseller", "Picker", "Thrifting", "MakingMoneyOnline", "WorkFromHome", "EbaySeller", or "SelfEmployeed". The goal of these hashtags is that people will search for them and find me.

Instagram allows you to include one website link in your profile; so, if you are using Instagram to bring in Ebay customers, you'll want to make that link the link to your Ebay Store. And while you can include the link when you share a photo, it won't be active. Therefore, a tip is to put something like, "25% off sale going on right now in our Ebay store; direct link in profile @yourinstagramaccount. The "@" link will take users to your profile page where the active link to your Ebay Store will be. Then the user simply clicks on your Ebay Store URL, taking then straight to your Ebay listings.

Some sellers are also using Instagram to sell items directly, skipping Ebay altogether. There are now many sellers who will put up a picture of an item and offer it up for sale right on Instagram. All someone has to do is message the poster (Instagram has a "mailbox" system that allows users to message one another) to give them their email so the seller can send them a PayPal invoice.

Just like with Facebook, Twitter and Pinterest, you'll want to network with other Ebay sellers and even your customers by following them back on Instagram and "liking" their posts. Include the link to your Instagram page on your blog/website, package enclosures, and Facebook page. And share your Instagram link periodically on Facebook and Twitter. While I have a main "Ann Eckhart" Instagram account, I also have a second account dedicated specifically to my Ebay store.

YouTube: A blog/website. Facebook. Twitter. Pinterest. Instagram. Are you feeling overwhelmed? Take a deep breath and relax; no one expects you to master these social networking sites and techniques in one day. Take one at a time before moving on to the next one. Once you've mastered the second site, continue on to the third, and so on.

We've already covered the biggest sites Ebay sellers are using to drive sales and make more money, but there are still others you can use, including YouTube. Not only can you use YouTube to drive traffic to your Ebay listings, but you can also make money on your videos through Google's AdSense program.

But what kind of videos can you make that will actually help you increase your Ebay sales?

One way to use YouTube to help sell your Ebay items is to take videos of products you have listed and include those videos in your Ebay listings. And you can also share the video via your other social media accounts in the hope that viewers will click through to the actual listing.

Note that making videos can be time-consuming, so shooting a video for every single item you have listed would likely not be worth it, especially for lower priced items. However, for items you are selling that have moving parts, play music, or are higher priced, adding a video to the listing may help sell it.

Under every YouTube video is a description box where you can include information as well as links. I include the links to my Amazon Author Page, blog, and all social media accounts under my videos so that viewers can easily click on the links to visit my various sites.

What many Ebay sellers do to grow their sales via YouTube is to make videos showing new inventory they will be listing. I do weekly haul videos on my YouTube channel showing all of the items I picked up at estate sales and thrift stores that I'll be selling on Ebay. Not only does this help educate others about how they can make money on Ebay, but it also lets customers know what items will be showing up in my Ebay store soon.

More than driving sales, however, making videos about your Ebay business is really about connecting with other sellers. Selling on Ebay can be a bit lonely when you don't know anyone else who does it. And chances are your friends and family don't understand what you do (or they just want you to sell their stuff for them). By sharing your Ebay business through YouTube videos and by searching out others, you'll quickly find yourself networking will fellow sellers. And once you connect on YouTube, you can also connect on Facebook, Twitter, and the other social networks.

You may think Ebay sellers are in competition with one another, but I've found the opposite to be true. People who sell on Ebay love meeting others who do, too. They enjoy watching YouTube videos about selling on Ebay, and they support each other on social networking.

And if you, like me, source secondhand items to resell on Ebay (from thrift stores, garage sales, and estate sales), YouTube is a fantastic resource to learn what items to look for to make money. When I transitioned from selling new gift items to secondhand goods, it was YouTube videos that helped teach me what items to look for when I was out "picking".

You don't need a fancy camera or high-price editing software to make YouTube videos. I actually film mine on an iPhone! After you upload a video, you can monetize it so that in brings in AdSense revenue. And once your video goes live, you can share it to social media via the convenient "share" icons YouTube provides under each video.

I make all kinds of Ebay related videos, including the hauls I mentioned earlier. I've also filmed lots of how-to videos teaching people everything from how to list items to what shipping materials I use.

For more information about YouTube, be sure to check out my book **How to Start a YouTube Channel for Fun & Profit** (the link to my Amazon Author Page is at the end of this book).

Tumblr: Tumblr is a micro-blogging and social networking site that allows you to share content that is somewhat similar to Pinterest in that you can create original posts or share the posts of others. There are some people, mostly celebrities and brands, who use Tumblr as their blog with it acting as their main landing page.

There are a lot of bloggers and brands on Tumblr, giving it a sort-of magazine feel. It's free and easy to create an account; and most blogs as well as YouTube provide easy "share" buttons that allow to you quickly post your content to your Tumblr page.

You can get as fancy as you want with Tumblr, changing up the theme and design. And you can authorize Google, Twitter, Facebook, and Instagram to automatically connect with your Tumblr account to share content and find your friends.

So how can Tumblr work to increase your Ebay sales? I use Tumblr the same way I use Google +, which is as a free and easy "extra" in my social media arsenal. I don't spend much time on Tumblr other than to share my blog posts, YouTube videos, and Instagram photos. I have my settings so that these posts are all automatically shared, meaning I don't have to manually do it. I haven't spent much time seeking out followers or following others on the site; but I do get periodic notification that another user has started following me.

The main Ebay content that I share on Tumblr is my YouTube videos, which consist of hauls and tutorials. Since there isn't a "share" button to Tumblr on Ebay, if I wanted to post my Ebay listings, I would have to manually do it; and at this point I don't feel that the time and effort needed to do that would result in enough sales to make it worth my time.

LinkedIn: LinkedIn is a social networking site specifically for the business community. Rather than sharing family photos like you do on Facebook, you want to keep LinkedIn strictly professional by only sharing your business content such as blog posts and Tweets related to your Ebay business.

Creating a LinkedIn account is free and easy; and you can automatically connect your account with your other social networking sites. As with Facebook, LinkedIn allows you to connect with fellow users. You can search out friends and past co-workers. Think of LinkedIn as an online resume where you highlight your past accomplishments as well as sharing your current business activities.

As far as using LinkedIn to increase your Ebay sales, I lump it into the same models as Google + and Tumblr in that they are free and easy extras that allow me to share my content via the widest reach possible. I have my LinkedIn account set up so that my blog posts are automatically shared there. Those who've I've connected with on LinkedIn can then click through to my blog if interested; and from there, they can find my Ebay listings.

Does my LinkedIn activity bring me any Ebay customers? Not really. However, since it's free to create an account, it's something you should take the time to do to add to your social media presence. There are Ebay seller groups on LinkedIn that you may want to check out, too.

Putting It All Together: When you sell on Ebay, your first and foremost concern should be creating new Ebay listings, sourcing new inventory, answering customer questions, and shipping out orders. A good title, photos and description are key to creating an Ebay listing that will result in a sale. Think of social media as the final step in that listing creation process.

As I've mentioned several times before, Ebay makes it easy to share your listings to Facebook, Twitter and Pinterest via "share" buttons located in every active listing. After I finish creating a listing, I click on the active link and go to the upper right-hand side of the page where the "share" buttons are. I click through to each one and post my listings. Note that connecting your Ebay account to your social media networks is a one-time step; once you've set it up, they will remain linked. It only takes about 15 seconds to share a listing to all three sites, a little longer if I add in hashtags.

One tip is that if you are listing a large batch of items is to share each individually to Twitter and Pinterest but to hold off on Facebook. Why? I talked before about how Facebook likes to "hide" business page posts, only showing your page followers a limited number of posts. So, if you flood Facebook with link after link, Facebook is going to hide the majority of them from your followers' feeds. Instead, wait until you have finished listing for the day and then post a photo of the items you listed to Facebook with a link to your Ebay store. Facebook tends to show individual photos over direct links, so it's much more likely followers will actually see your photo and click through to your listings.

If you are using Instagram, try posting a photo at least a few times a week. You can upload shots of your office, new inventory, or even what you are having for lunch. Include three to five hashtags so that users can find you. And be sure you are following other users and "liking" their content, too. I like to spend a few minutes at the end of the day scrolling through my Instagram feed to connect with other users.

Having a blog/website and/or YouTube channel will add a considerable amount of more work for you, so only use them if you feel they are benefitting your sales or you are getting something from them personally (as in networking with other sellers). If you do utilize those options, be sure to share the content you create to all of your other social networking sites.

When I upload a new YouTube video, I share it to Facebook, Twitter, and Pinterest using the "share" buttons under the video; and I also post it to my blog. Again, that post then gets sent to readers who have signed up for the blog post alerts.

While I put in a lot of effort to market my Ebay Store online, I also have promotional tools I use offline. As I mentioned earlier, I include a packing slip in all of my Ebay orders (you can print these directly from PayPal after your shipping label has printed); and I also include a business card sized "thank you" note in all packages (I order these from VistaPrint). The cards contain my Ebay store URL in the hope customers will come back to shop with me. It also gives orders a personal touch that helps cultivate positive feedback.

While all of these additional social networking and marketing steps can seem overwhelming, trust me that after a while promotion efforts become second nature. The increase in sales, as well as the fun you'll have connecting with other Ebay sellers, will make the extra work worth it!

CHAPTER 5

COST-EFFECTIVE, TIME-SAVING SHIPPING TIPS & TRICKS

There is a lot more that goes into shipping Ebay orders than just putting items into a box and slapping on a shipping label. And shipping is the one thing that almost all new sellers struggle with. While finding items to resell and making money are the most fun parts of selling on Ebay, knowing how to properly ship items is essential.

In this chapter, I am going to go over everything you need to know to ship out orders on Ebay, from having the right supplies and the various shipping services, to setting up the shipping in each listing and packaging orders.

Printer: In order to ship orders quickly and for the least amount of money, you are going to want to print labels from home; so, having a printer to print labels is essential.

I use a LaserJet that prints black and white. It is fast, prints numerous pages from one toner cartridge, and it fits on my desk. While one toner cartridge costs about $70, I only need to purchase one a year. I print my labels out onto white copy paper, cut them along the border, and tape them to my packages.

If you are just starting to sell on Ebay and already have a printer, use it until you see a need to upgrade to a better model. Inkjet printers use a lot of expensive ink and you have to change the cartridges frequently. If you are going to be shipping out a few packages each day, you'll eventually want to upgrade your printer. I personally bought my current model, and HP LaserJet P1606dn, during a Black Friday sale at Staples when it was half off, paying less than $100 for it.

As your Ebay sales increase, you may look into a printer that prints shipping labels (the kind with the peel-off backs that you can just stick onto a package) or even a thermal printer. I have been selling on Ebay for over 10 years, and I am still fine using a LaserJet; however, you may eventually determine that a printer dedicated to shipping labels is better for you.

Digital Scale: The number one supply you MUST have if you are going to sell on Ebay is a digital scale to weigh packages. You can buy digital scales for around $20 on Ebay, and they are also sold at office supply stores and on Amazon.

You don't need a fancy model, just a scale that weighs ounces and pounds. I have had the same digital scale for over seven years now; it's an investment you MUST make if you are going to ship your Ebay orders yourself. If you aren't willing to purchase a digital scale for your Ebay shipping, then you should stop reading this book and resign yourself to hauling all of your packages to the Post Office.

I have encountered many sellers over the years who sell on Ebay without a scale. They estimate the shipping, overcharging customers in some cases (and getting negative feedback) or undercharging and losing money. Or they take all items to the Post Office BEFORE listing them to get a weight, list them, and then go BACK to the Post Office for postage after they sell. That, to me, is a HUGE waste of time and gas money!

I also see many sellers charging all customers one flat rate for shipping, which is another big mistake. Buyers come to Ebay for deals, and the shipping charges factor into that. As I stated above, charging one flat rate will result in overcharging some customers and undercharging others. However, if you offer CALCULATED SHIPPING, the buyer pays the actual shipping cost based on the weight of the package and the zip code it is going to. If you have a digital scale on hand, using calculated shipping is a breeze. I will talk more about calculated shipping later on in this chapter.

Other sellers offer "free" shipping, padding the cost of the item into their estimated shipping charge. While offering free shipping is a smart move for lightweight items (for instance, if you have a piece of jewelry that weighs 2-ounces, you can easily offer free shipping and absorb the $1 it will cost to ship), it can backfire on heavier items as buyers know when a seller has inflated the price of an item to cover shipping. You don't want to give the appearance that you are making money from the shipping costs and risk getting negative feedback.

Instead of guessing the postage costs or running back and forth to the Post Office, you can save time and money by easily printing your shipping labels from home....and a digital scale makes that possible!

Boxes & Envelopes: You can't just stick a label directly on a book and send it in the mail (although, sadly, some new sellers do this). Shipping requires shipping supplies, and that means shipping boxes and envelopes.

The great thing about the United States Postal Service (USPS) is that they offer FREE Priority Mail shipping boxes (I will be talking a lot more about Priority Mail and the other forms of shipping services coming up). While Priority Mail is a great option for shipping most packages, you will need other forms of packaging for Media Mail, First Class Mail and Parcel Select, as well as for international shipments. Basically, you need two forms of shipping boxes/envelopes: Priority Mail boxes and envelopes for Priority Mail, and plain boxes and envelopes for Media Mail, First Class Mail, and Parcel Select.

Before you run out and buy new shipping boxes and envelopes, check around your house to see what you have on hand. Plain cardboard boxes, manila envelopes, and bubble mailers can all be used for non-Priority mail. If you already have items on hand you that you will be listing on Ebay, look them over to determine the packaging you need. Perhaps you are only going to sell books, for which bubble mailers and sturdy boxes are enough. However, if you only plan to sell large items, you don't need to worry about stocking up on envelopes.

I keep a wide variety of boxes and envelopes on hand. While I utilize the free Priority Mail boxes and bubble mailers from the Post Office, I do invest in nice shipping materials from Amazon, Ebay, Uline, ValueMailers, and Sam's Club.

However, because I have been selling on Ebay for years and am set up as a business, these are items I can buy and then deduct as business expenses. If you are just starting out, use what you already have on hand; and don't be shy about asking your friends and family for any boxes they may have. With more and more people shopping online, many people have accumulated cardboard boxes they are desperate to get rid of. I save every box that I myself get a shipment in. I often order online from Amazon, and their boxes are a great size for shipping oddly shaped items such as board games.

If you are using repurposed boxes, be sure to use a marker to black out any writing on the outside of the box. You want to neatly cover up any company names or other information on the outside. I always pick up the thick black Sharpies when I see them on sale for this very purpose.

Also, do not wrap your boxes in brown wrapping paper. This is something I see a lot of new Ebay sellers do, but it is completely unnecessary. Not only is it a waste of time and money, the Post Office actually prefers that you do NOT wrap your boxes as the paper can become lodged in the sorting machines.

Packing Materials: You can't just throw an item into a box and ship it as is (well, you CAN, as I have seen many sellers do; but you shouldn't). You need to WRAP up your items to protect them inside of the box. Again, since I have an established Ebay business, I invest in recycled packing paper to wrap up the items. However, I then use newspapers to further protect the item. Do NOT wrap your item in the newspaper directly; you don't want any newspaper ink to bleed onto your products.

In addition to packing paper, I also purchase bubble wrap. In my area, I have found Sam's Club to have the best price on bubble wrap. Bubble wrap is a MUST for protecting ceramics such as coffee mugs (of which I sell a lot of!). Again, after the item is wrapped securely in bubble wrap, I then use newspaper to further buffer it inside of the box.

Packing peanuts are always nice to have on hand to use in shipments, but buying them new is expensive. I save any that I get from online orders I myself place, and I let my friends and family know that I will gladly take their unwanted packing peanuts off of their hands. Most people are happy to get rid of the packing peanuts they have as they are a static mess to deal with.

Packing Tape: So, you now have boxes, envelopes, packing paper, newspaper, bubble wrap, and maybe even some packing peanuts. In order to close up your packages, you need packing tape. Clear packing tape can be found at the drugstores, big box retailers, office supply stores, warehouse clubs, and even the dollar stores. I purchase my packing tape at either Staples or Sam's Club. A case of Staples brand tape is $30 and lasts me a year; the Mead brand that Staples sells contains six large rolls and lasts several months.

I also have a red handheld tape dispenser (sold right next to the tape). If you are just starting out, I recommend you buy a kit with the tape dispenser and some extra tape rolls. You can usually find such a kit for $10-15 in the tape section. You only need to buy the dispenser once and then tape refills as needed. Buy the best quality tape dispenser and tape you can as you will use less. Cheap tape isn't a good deal if you have to use more of it to seal up packages.

Shipping Station: Now that you have all of your shipping supplies, you need a place to prepare your shipments. If you have the space, it's nice to designate an area for shipping. I have a table in my office where my digital scale always sits at the ready. It's right next to my computer so that I can weigh items as I am listing them (again, lots more on this coming up). The most important thing is to have your digital scale on a flat surface so that you can get an accurate reading.

I have shelving for all of my boxes, envelopes, packing materials, and tape. Again, since I have an established business, I have a lot of materials. However, if you are just starting out, use an out-of-the-way space (perhaps in the basement) for your shipping supplies. You want to make sure your supplies (and the items you are selling) are away from any smoke, pets or other household odors. Yes, customers WILL complain if they find dog hair inside of their packages; and complaints about cigarette smoke can lead to negative feedback.

Package Categories: Now for the most confusing part of selling on Ebay: the shipping categories. There are dozens of carriers and ways you can ship packages. While UPS and FedEx are viable shipping options, you'll want to ship most of your packages shipping through the United States Postal Service (USPS). The USPS provides the best value and service for small sellers, and Ebay has partnered with them to make shipping easy and cost-effective. Since the USPS is Ebay's preferred shipping partner, if you sell on Ebay, you will be using them a lot.

While there are dozens of ways you can ship a package through the Post Office, in this section I am going to focus on the four main ways you will likely ship your Ebay packages: Media Mail, First Class Mail, Parcel Select, and Priority Mail. These four options are all for packages being shipped within the United States. When you are just starting out, save yourself any confusion and only focus on these shipping categories.

Media Mail: Media Mail is for, surprise, MEDIA! It is preferable to send books via Media Mail because they are heavy and you get a discounted rate. However, the low price also means that Media Mail is extremely slow, sometimes taking up to one month (although the Post Office claims delivery is two to eight business days).

The following items qualify to be shipped via Media Mail:

- Books of at least eight printed pages

- 16-millimeter or narrower width films and catalogs of films 24 pages or more

- Printed music

- Educational testing materials and printed educational materials

- Sound recordings

- Play scripts and manuscripts

- Loose-leaf pages and their binders of education medical information

- Computer-readable media

Media Mail can NOT be used for advertising, video games, computer drives, or digital drives. The maximum weight for a Media Mail package is 70-pounds.

Some sellers try to cheat the system by shipping heavy, non-media items via Media Mail. This is a violation of USPS policy and can result in you losing your postal account. Post offices are notorious for opening Media Mail boxes to make sure they only contain approved media items, so be careful to follow the rules.

Media Mail items can only be shipped in plain boxes or envelopes, not in the Priority Mail boxes. When you print a label via Ebay (more on how to do this coming up), it will clearly state on the label which service you paid for. So, if you print a Media Mail label, it will say "MEDIA MAIL" at the top.

First Class Mail: First Class Mail is the service you use when you send a letter. One stamp equals one ounce; and you can ship up to 16-ounces (one pound) via First Class. Just like Media Mail, First Class packages must be in plain boxes or envelopes; you cannot use the free Priority Mail boxes or envelopes to ship First Class packages.

Shipping items via First Class is where having a postal scale really comes in handy as you can get your package down to the exact ounce. Every ounce means more money spent, so it's important to get as close of a weight on your item as possible (I'll talk more about weighing your packages coming up). If you are using calculated shipping and having your customers pay the shipping charge, being able to offer them First Class Mail saves them money. If the package you are sending weighs 10 ounces, the difference between First Class and Parcel or Priority can be as much as $3.

However, even with a digital scale, finding the exact ounce can be hard as you need an item weight before you list an item. My trick, and one that I will talk more about later in this book, is to add three-ounces to the weight of all packages to account for packing materials. So, if you have a small item that on its own weighs six-ounces, list it as nine-ounces. That way when it is in an envelope with a packing slip, you won't risk the Post Office sending it back for insufficient postage.

Parcel Select: Parcel Select, formerly called Parcel Post, is for packages weighing over 16-ounces. Parcel is slower than Priority (shipping time can take up to two weeks, although the Post Office claims two to eight business days), but it is cheaper for heavy shipments. Parcel shipments must be in plain boxes or envelopes; just as with Media Mail and First Class, you can't ship Parcel Select shipments in the Priority Mail boxes.

The cost of Parcel Select postage depends on the weight of the package and where it is going to. That is why it is smart to use Ebay's Calculated Shipping as the customer pays for the exact shipping for their zip code.

While Parcel Select is a great option for heavy packages, you want to make sure to double check the cost between Parcel and Priority when you are creating your shipping label through Ebay (again, I will be going over how to do this coming up). Depending on how far away the package is going, Priority Mail may be the cheaper option.

As an example, I am in Iowa, centrally located from both coasts in the middle of the country. For packages weighing less than four pounds, it is often cheaper for me to ship via Priority Mail over Parcel Select. Plus, I get to use a Priority free box, and I get a discount on postage by shipping directly through Ebay.

What is great about shipping through Ebay is that you can look at all of the package and price options before paying for and printing a label. So, you can find the best rate for your shipment. It's always nice when a customer pays for Parcel but then you can upgrade them to Priority. Not only do you save money, but the item arrives much faster. Don't worry, I will be going over how to do this in Section 4!

Of course, this brings up the issue of overcharging the buyer. Now, if a customer pays for Parcel but I am able to give him Priority for a dollar or two less, I don't worry about the difference. I know that the buyer will view Priority shipping as an upgrade on my part, which will result in great feedback for me. The bit of money I "make" from the difference will just go towards my packing supplies. However, if the difference is several dollars or more, I will refund the buyer the difference. Again, since everything goes through PayPal, issuing a partial refund is easy and will make the buyer very happy!

The maximum weight for a Parcel package is 70 pounds.

Priority Mail: Priority Mail is for packages weighing over 16-ounces that need to get to their location quickly, typically two to three business days. Note that "business days" means weekdays and doesn't include Saturdays and Sundays. If you ship an item out on a Friday, it may not be processed at the Post Office until Monday. From there, it will have an additional two to three days before it reaches the customer.

As I explained above when talking about Parcel Select, sometimes Priority Mail can be the cheaper option. For me, this is often true for packages weighing less than four pounds that are going as far as the East coast. I also get a shipping discount because I ship directly through Ebay, and I get the Priority Mail boxes for free. In fact, the vast majority of my shipments go via Priority Mail as nine times out of 10 it ends up being the cheapest option for packages between one and four pounds.

Priority Mail has other bonuses over Parcel Select including FREE tracking when you purchase the label online, Saturday delivery, and FREE Carrier Pickup. I utilize Carrier Pickup to have my mail lady pick up my packages; in order to have her take my packages; however, I have to have at least one Priority Mail package. If I have all Parcel Select packages, for example, I can't request the free pickup. Since I work from home, Carrier Pickup is a blessing as I don't have to make multiple trips to the Post Office every week!

Of course, the best thing about Priority Mail is the FREE boxes! There are many sizes of Priority Mail boxes, including Regular, Flat Rate, and Regional options. Unless you are only selling clothing, which fits easily into poly mailers, you'll want to stock up on all of the various sizes of Priority Mail boxes the Post Office offers. Your mail carrier will even deliver them to you for FREE!

While the Post Office promotes their Flat Rate boxes as the best price, for packages less than four pounds, Regular Priority Mail is usually cheaper. Why? When it comes to Priority Mail, it's not just the weight but also the distance a package has to travel.

As I mentioned previously, I live in Iowa. I can send a two-pound package to Minnesota for a little more than $6. However, that same package costs over $11 to ship to California. If that package is going to New York, the postage is around $9. To Hawaii or Alaska, the cost jumps to $14. Again, it's not just the weight but the distance the package has to travel.

The type of Priority Mail box (Regular, Flat Rate or Regional) doesn't affect the speed of delivery. Priority is Priority. The difference in the shipping cost depends on the type and size of the box.

Regular Priority Mail: A regular Priority Mail box is priced by weight and the zip code to which it is being shipped. You can ship Priority Mail packages in regular boxes and envelopes, too, not only in the branded Priority boxes.

The maximum weight for a Priority Mail package is 70 pounds. If using your own box, note that the maximum combined length and girth is 108-inches, which means the combined measurement of the longest side and the distance around the thickest part of the package can't be more than 108-inches.

The Post Office provides FREE Priority Mail stickers to put on plain boxes and envelopes. I keep rolls of stickers on hand for when we ship Priority packages in plain boxes and envelopes.

Flat Rate Priority Mail: Flat Rate boxes have a set price. You can pack them up to 70-pounds and pay one flat rate no matter where the package is going. However, there are various sizes of Flat Rate boxes and envelopes, each with its own price. The Post Office is constantly raising prices; but as of this writing, the envelopes and small boxes start at around $6, the medium boxes ship for a bit over $12, and the large box ships for a bit over $17. The price varies depending on whether you print the labels yourself online (cheaper) or have them printed at the Post Office (more expensive).

While the Post Office heavily promotes Flat Rate boxes as the best option, Flat Rate is often times more expensive than shipping via regular Priority. For instance, say you have a ceramic dish that weighs four pounds once it is in a shipping box. If you put it in a Flat Rate box, it will cost over $12 to ship anywhere in the country. Now, if you are in Florida and your buyer is in California that works out to be a great deal. However, if your buyer lives in your state or in a surrounding one, you'll pay much less in shipping by choosing Regular Priority.

Again, by using Ebay's shipping tool, you will be able to see and compare all of the options available so that you can find the best deal (and I will show you how to do this in Section 4). However, note that if a customer pays for Priority, you need to ship the item Priority. Priority is an Expedited Service and is the fastest option as compared to Media, First Class or Parcel. So, if your buyer pays for Priority and you downgrade them to Parcel, they are rightfully going to be angry.

Regional Priority Mail: Regional boxes are a new offering from the Post Office. There are three different sizes available: A1, A2, and B. I have found that the A1 and A2 boxes are often cheaper than the Regular Priority Mail boxes for the shipments I do.

The downsides to Regional Rate are that the boxes themselves are on the smaller size and they have lower weight limits (15 pounds for the A and 20 pounds for the B box. However, I keep a supply on hand in case I find that they are the best option. Again, since I ship online via Ebay, I can look at all of the shipping options before purchasing a label in order to choose the best option.

More About Priority Mail: When packages are being sorted for shipment at the Post Office, the most expensive postage options go first as they are guaranteed space on the trucks and planes. Overnight is obviously the most expensive since the customer is paying for next day delivery. Media Mail and Bulk Mail (bulk mail is usually junk mail that is sent out in mass) are the cheapest and therefore the last packages to be put out for delivery. It's all about available space; the more room on the truck or plane, the more packages they will ship out.

The Post Office promotes Priority Mail as being delivered in two to three business days. Again, that is BUSINESS days, i.e. WEEKDAYS. While some facilities process mail on the weekends, most do not.

After Priority, First Class Mail is shipped out, then Parcel Select, and finally Media Mail. It's always in your best interest as a seller to use the fastest option available depending on the price. The faster the customer receives their order, the happier they will be!

Carrier Pickup: If you are at home when your mail carrier comes, using Carrier Pick-up is a huge time and money saver. It takes me a good hour to make the round trip to my Post Office, including the time I spend standing in line. Using Carrier Pick-up means my packages are picked up and sometimes even scanned right on my doorstep!

As long as you have at least one Priority Mail package to be picked up, you can request Carrier Pick-up for all of your packages. You need to place the request online the night before. If you have a smart phone, the USPS Mobile App makes this incredibly easy to do, although you can do it online as well.

If you live in a safe and relatively secluded area, you might be able to set your packages outside for your carrier to pick up. When I lived in a condo in the country, I was able to do this. However, when I moved to a house on a busy street in town, my packages were stolen off of my front porch twice; so, I've had to put on my request form for my carrier to ring the doorbell when she arrives so that I can hand her the packages.

If you do use Carrier Pick-up, make things easier on your carrier by putting your packages in a large bag or box (you can pick up plastic tubs from the Post Office). If I have a lot of packages, my carrier will often drive her truck into the driveway and I will help her load the packages into the back.

Be as helpful as you can to your carrier if you are utilizing pick-up; and thank them at the holidays with a nice card and a $10 gift card (the maximum amount allowed by the Post Office). This year I gave my carrier a $10 Cold Stone Creamery gift card, which she absolutely loved! In the past, I've given her gift cards to Starbucks and Target. Picking up all of my packages adds a lot to her work load, so a small token of thanks is well deserved!

Global Shipping: Shipping items internationally is very lucrative but it used to be so confusing that many Ebay sellers, even those who had been on the site for years, avoided it. However, now shipping to customers across the globe is incredibly easy through Ebay's Global Shipping program.

I have to admit that I was a bit skeptical of Global Shipping when it was first introduced. The idea of shipping orders to a central sorting facility where Ebay would then assume all responsibility for shipping the package to the international customer sounded too good to be true, and I feared that Ebay would screw it up. I was initially put into the program automatically, but I opted out. I was then opted in AGAIN, but that time I decided to stay and give it a shot.

Fortunately, I have been pleasantly surprised by the ease and success I have had using Global Shipping! Customers pay me the domestic shipping cost to send the item to Ebay's facility. From there, Ebay takes full responsibility for getting it to the international customer, including handling all customs forms. I used to spend so much time filling out those stupid forms, but now I don't have to mess with them!

Since opting into Global Shipping (or being opted into it!), my international sales have increased without any extra effort on my part. There are millions upon millions of Ebay customers all over the world; and with Global Shipping, you can sell to them just as easily as you would to someone in your own city!

CHAPTER 6

TIPS & TRICKS FOR MANAGING AN EBAY STORE

Many sellers think having an Ebay Store is all about the customer's experience. But the truth is that sellers gain a lot more from a store in terms of reduced fees and organization than buyers do from shopping in a "store" setting. Because most customers will find your listings in Ebay's search, many will not even click through to your actual Ebay Store. But even though most buyers won't venture into your "store" doesn't mean you shouldn't have one!

Store vs. No Store: One of the most common questions I get about selling on Ebay is whether or not to open a store. The general rule of thumb is that if you are consistently going to have at least 100 items listed on Ebay, then a store makes the most financial sense.

There are currently five store levels on Ebay:

- **Starter:** $4.95 a month for 100 fixed-price listings

- **Basic:** $21.95 a month for 250 fixed-price listings

- **Premium:** $59.95 a month for 1,000 fixed-price listings

- **Anchor:** $299.95 a month for 10,000 fixed-price listings

- **Enterprise:** $2,999.95 a month for 100,000 fixed-price listings

Each store subscription also offers different levels of fee discounts, including listing (once you've gone over the allotted number included in your subscription) and final value fees. Basic stores and higher also receive a quarterly coupon from Ebay to put towards Ebay branded shipping supplies. I have a Premium store subscription, so I receive $50 every three months to spend on poly bags, tape, boxes, tissue paper, and stickers. That $200 a year credit really helps keep my overall shipping supply costs low.

New sellers often feel that they have to get their Ebay store "ready" before opening it to the public. However, you need to remember that an Ebay store isn't like a brick-and-mortar store. The vast majority of customers will access your listings in Ebay's search, not through your actual store. It will only be after you start promoting your Store URL (more on this next) that people will actually get to your storefront to see what you have for sale.

You don't need to worry about having the perfect store right out of the gate or commit to a large subscription. You can sign up for a Starter store, and then work on it gradually. While I encourage you to have a great store design, your first priority should be getting your items listed. If you find that things are going well, you can always upgrade your subscription level; in fact, Ebay will likely message you with special offers to upgrade your store if it is performing well. Note, however, that while it's easy to upgrade to a larger store, it can be difficult to downgrade as the store pricing if for one year. So, if you decide to downgrade early, you could face paying the difference in the store subscription cost.

Store Name: I recommend you make your Ebay user name the same as your store name. You want to "brand" yourself and your business, and having both names match helps with that (as does making sure all of your business social networking sites also have the same name).

Choose a professional sounding name; you want to make sure nothing in your store name is offensive to potential buyers.

Store URL: There are a lot of positives to having an Ebay store, and one of the best is that it provides you with a dedicated URL (website) address. It can be very hard to find a seller's listings based only on their screen name (Ebay seems to be constantly moving the seller search feature), but it's easy to give your customers your Ebay Store URL. Your store URL is easy to find as it will be in the web address bar whenever you are looking at your storefront.

If you have an Ebay Store, you will want to include your store URL on enclosures and on your social media sites so that customers only have to click on the link to be taken to your storefront. Website companies such as GoDaddy make purchasing a URL incredibly easy and provide step-by-step instructions for redirecting that URL to your Ebay store.

For years, I had dedicated URL's that pointed to my Ebay store. They were simply dot com names for my business, as opposed to the longer direct store URL that Ebay provides. I registered the URL's via GoDaddy, and it was a lot easier to give people the shorter dot come name than the Ebay address.

Store Design: Ebay allows you to customize the look and layout of your Ebay store, which unfortunately few sellers seem to do. Why spend the extra money to have a store but not spend a few minutes making it look its best? After all, you are hoping that customers will come to your Ebay store to see everything you have for sale, so be sure to make it look as nice as possible. You can choose a color scheme, add in your logo, and customize promotion boxes.

I access my store design dashboard by going to my store homepage and clicking on the "Manage My Store" icon at the top or bottom of the page (depending on what internet browser I am using). I am taken to a screen where all the options to edit my store are available. On the left-hand side is a menu of all the choices for personalization.

Something very important you should do with your store is to load up the store description area (the rectangular area at the top of the page) with as many keywords as possible in order for your store to be picked up by search engines. In mine, I welcome shoppers to my store and let them know all of the categories I sell in. I cram in as many category keywords as I can into that space!

Store Categories: One of the advantages of having an Ebay store is the ability to create specific item categories. Not only can buyers narrow down their search when they are looking at your store, but it is helpful for you as a seller to keep track of your inventory.

The great thing about categories is you can add and delete them as you see fit. Perhaps you have a large stock of camera equipment to sell so you create a "Camera" category. However, after you have sold all of the cameras, you can delete the "Camera" category or simply leave it in your store set up as only categories with active listings show up. Inactive categories will still be visible to you in the "Manage Your

Store" section, but they will only be seen by customers if or when you add items to them.

I like to arrange my categories alphabetically. While you can break down categories into subcategories, unless you have thousands of items listed, you are usually fine simply listing in the main category.

Make sure to properly spell and capitalize your categories. I like to put mine in all capitals such as "COLLECTIBLES" and "COFFEE MUGS". I personally think typing a category like "BIBLES & HYMNALS" looks a lot better than "bibles and hymnals".

Once you have an Ebay store, you will be able to select the store categories for your items whenever you go to list something. You can list in two store categories. Note that the store categories are different from the Ebay categories, where you get one free and have to pay for a second.

Promotion Boxes: Ebay store sellers have the ability to add Promotion Boxes to their store design. Ebay provides pre-designed ones with options for newly listed or ending soon items as well as the option for customers to sign up for a newsletter.

I usually have two promotion boxes at the top of my store, one for newly listed items and one for the store newsletter. I also add a promotion box to the left side of my store, under the categories, where I have my Terms of Service spelled out.

As with all store features, you can change your promotion boxes at any time. I think it is nice to go in once and awhile to change the look of your promotion boxes as it keeps your store design fresh!

Listing Frame: Did you know that you can add your store design to all of your active listings, whether or not a customer is looking at your store or not? This option is called the "Listing Frame", and you will find the link under the "Edit Store" option on the left-hand side of the screen under the "Manage My Store" section that I talked about earlier.

Adding in the "Listing Frame" means all of your listings will show your storefront navigation in them, meaning your store header and store categories will be accessible to anyone looking at your listings. This is an easy way for you to drive traffic to your other listings as people can quickly go to your store. You can customize exactly what you want your listing frame to look like, and you can even add options for buyers to be added to your newsletter list and to add you as a favorite seller.

Vacation Mode: If you have an Ebay store and sales are slow, a little trick you can use is to put your Ebay Store on vacation. Vacation mode is only available to people with Ebay stores. You can choose to either hide your listings completely or leave them visible on the site. Either way, a message will appear letting customers know you are currently away. You can even this message if you want to.

If you choose to make your items remain visible, people can still buy them but Ebay lets them know that there may be a delay in shipping them. I always choose to hide my listings completely, though, because even under vacation mode, if someone buys an item, they can still leave you negative feedback or ding your stars if they don't get their package during the regularly stated delivery time.

Whichever version you choose, when you take your listings off of vacation mode, they will likely get rebooted in the Ebay system and will show up as newly listing items. While there is no official word from Ebay that this is true, most sellers report that they see a spike in sales after putting their store on vacation. If sales are absolutely dead, I will put my store on vacation overnight; and I have always gotten sales when I reactivated my listings the following day. I refer to this as "jiggling my store switch"!

Vacation mode only works on Fixed Price listings, not on Auctions. Also, it takes a little while for your listings to change over to the vacation settings, usually around half an hour. It takes about the same amount of time to reactivate them when you are ready.

If I have an actual vacation planned (i.e. I am not just doing the Ebay store jiggle trick!), I make sure that all of my auctions are ending at least a week beforehand so that buyers have time to pay and I have time to ship. When I am down to only Fixed Price listings, I will put my store on vacation a few days ahead of time so that I have time to ship out any orders I may get. After all, I don't want to have to be wrapping up a package while trying to make my flight!

Promotions Manager: Another great feature you can access when you have an Ebay store is the ability to run promotions such as sales and special discounts through Promotions Manager (formerly called "Markdown Manager"). There are five distinct offers you can set up under the Promotions Manager:

- **Order discounts**: Offer discounts based on order size, or the amount spent by a buyer. You can also create promotions such as a percentage off an additional item, or buy one get one free

- **Codeless coupons**: Offer exclusive discounts to buyer groups of your choosing by using a virtual coupon

- **Promotional shipping**: Offer cheaper shipping on items that qualify for your offer

- **Sales events**: Reduce prices for selected items or categories

- **Volume price discounts**: Offer tiered discounts to buyers who purchase multiple quantities of a single item

To access the Promotions Manager, simply go to your **Seller Hub** and click on the **Marketing** tab at the top of the page. Once on the **Manage promotions** page, click on Promotions on the left side of the page. Then click on the **Create a promotion** tab on the right side of page and choose from:

- Order discount

- Shipping discount

- Volume pricing

- Codeless coupon

- Sale event + markdown

You'll definitely want to explore each option to understand how they work, but the most popular is Sale event + markdown, which is how you run a sale in your Ebay store. Sale event + markdown offers sellers three options:

- Take a percentage off of each item you select

- Take a specific dollar amount off of each item you select

- Offer free shipping for all discounted items (will apply to all of the items that you put on sale)

Running a percentage or dollar off sale is the most commonly used technique Ebay sellers use to drive traffic to their listings. You can choose when you want your sale to start as well as when you want it to end; and you can select which listings you want to include. It usually takes a few hours after setting up a sale for the markdown to actually be applied to your listings. If you make a mistake or want to cancel the sale, you can easily edit or cancel your sale at any time, even after the sale has started.

I personally run sales anywhere from 5% to 50% off, depending on the item and how long I've had it. I like to start sales on Saturday mornings and run them through Friday nights; letting sales end and then launching new ones can help refresh your listings on Ebay's site, which can lead to them appearing higher in search.

Whichever you choose, percentage or dollar amount, the item will appear on Ebay's site with a "SALE" icon. The original price will be crossed out (but still visible) and the sale price will be next to it.

Promoted Listings: As if the store fees, listing fees, and final value fees aren't enough, Ebay now offers sellers the opportunity to pay for Promoted Listings. With Promoted Listings, you pay an additional Ebay fee if a buyer purchases an item that was promoted. For instance, let's say you have a shirt listed and your customer sees it at the top of the page (it will be marked as "Sponsored") when they are searching for tops. If they purchase the shirt marked as "Sponsored", you'll then pay a percentage of the sale to Ebay (this amount will be added to your overall Ebay fees for the month).

Note that just because you may choose to promote ALL of your listings doesn't mean that you'll have to pay the percentage fee on all of your sales. That's because not all promoted items appear in search. Let's go back to the shirt example I used earlier. Say your customer was searching through the shirt listings; there were a few at the top that were promoted, but yours was down further on the page. Because other sellers paid for a higher promoted spot, their tops appeared before yours; but the buyer ended up purchasing from you, even though that listing didn't appear to them as promoted (it wasn't marked as "Sponsored").

An easier way to look at this is to think that each of your listings are appearing twice on Ebay's site, both as a promoted listing and as a non-promoted listing. What one customer sees in their Ebay feed is different from what another buyer sees. Your buyer might see your promoted listing (marked as "Sponsored") and purchase it, meaning you'll pay the additional fee. However, another seller might NOT see your listing as being promoted (i.e. NOT marked as "Sponsored") and still purchase it, meaning you DON'T pay the additional fee on that sale.

Fortunately, you can choose your percentage when setting up a Promoted Listing campaign. Some sellers only run their promotions at the 1% rate, while others choose the trending rate, which varies by category and can exceed 10%. I prefer to set one low percentage rate across all of my listings. I also run my Promoted Listings for one week at a time; just like starting and ending sales, letting Promoted Listings end and then starting new campaigns can help your listings refresh on Ebay's site.

You can access the Promoted Listings page in the **Seller Hub** under **Marketing**. Simply click on the **Create a new campaign icon** to explore this feature. You can select your listings individually or in bulk. After your campaign goes live, you can then adjust the date you want it to end; and you can also end it manually if you change your mind.

CHAPTER 7

CUSTOMER SERVICE TIPS & TRICKS

One of the biggest features that makes selling on Ebay different from other ecommerce websites is the Feedback system. Customers can not only leave sellers three different levels of Feedback, but they can also rate them on communication and shipping. And the feedback and ratings you get affect what, if any, listing discounts and selling privileges you receive. Therefore, you must provide stellar customer service in order to ensure positive feedback.

Communication: One mistake I see new sellers make is that they are overzealous when it comes to communicating with their buyers. I know sellers who send their buyers multiple messages, which is not only unnecessary but really annoying. Unless there is a problem, the only communication you need to initiate with customers is to send them an invoice for their item, which you do through Ebay on your My Ebay page. Simply select "Send Invoice" from the drop-down menu next to the item.

If you are shipping online through Ebay, the buyer will get a notice from Ebay with the package tracking information when you have shipped their package; so, there is no need to send them another message letting them know their item has shipped.

I only contact a customer if they haven't paid, and in that message, I give them a "friendly reminder" that their payment is due. If they don't pay, I initiate a claim through Ebay. I don't send buyers a message immediately after they make a purchase demanding payment as Ebay gives buyers four days to submit payment. I don't send buyers messages asking for feedback. And I don't send messages thanking them for their order. The only communication I have with my customers outside of the Ebay invoicing and tracking systems is through the enclosures I put in their packages.

Terms of Service: Making your terms of service clear to buyers will go a long way towards avoiding any complications or complaints.

Many new sellers "threaten" buyers in their listings, telling them they must submit payment immediately. When setting up an Ebay account, all users agree to Ebay's terms, which are that buyers have four days to pay. Not only are these "threats" baseless, but they will turn potential customers off.

Returns: Whether or not to accept returns is a decision only you can make. Be sure to fill out the **Return options** section within your listings; it's located right above the "Shipping details" field. You'll need to check or uncheck the boxes next to both domestic and international orders to designate if you accept returns or not. If you choose to accept returns, more fields will pop up so that you can further set your policies, including if you or the customer will pay the return postage and how long the buyer has to return the item. You can also bulk edit your listings to set your return policies.

For years, I accepted returns with buyers paying the return shipping costs. However, as online shopping increased and customers became used to the liberal return policies offered by major retailers, my returns grew to a point where I just couldn't afford to accept them any longer.

I currently do NOT accept returns unless there is an issue with the item, such as a flaw I missed.

Ebay allows sellers to deny returns completely UNLESS the item is damaged or not as described. Sellers who do not accept returns do NOT have to take back items simply due to the buyer changing their mind. However, ALL sellers, regardless of their return policies, have to accept returns for items that are damaged or items not as described (i.e. "INAD"). While most buyers are honest, there are of course some who like to cheat Ebay's system by claiming an item wasn't as described (INAD) in order to force a return, even though they simply have buyer's remorse.

In these situations, you'll likely have to call Ebay to see if they will back you on the issue. Unfortunately, Ebay has a history of siding with buyers in these cases unless you can prove without a shadow of a doubt that you are in the right. For instance, I recently sold a shirt that was brand new with tags. The customer wanted to return it for fit. Even though I don't accept returns, it was a higher priced item, so I decided to make an exception. However, when I got the shirt back, I saw that the customer had cut off the tag, meaning I could no longer sell the top as new with tags. I reached out to Ebay but was told that I couldn't prove that the buyer had cut the tag off. So, not only did I have to issue a full refund to the customer, I was left with a lower quality item.

Ebay has also started pressuring sellers to offer "free returns", meaning that customers can return an item and the seller has to pay for the return shipping cost. As a small seller, I personally can't afford to cover the return postage on items, especially since I typically offer free shipping on the initial order. Sellers who do offer "free returns" are usually high-volume businesses who can absorb the costs.

Free shipping, no returns, free returns; there are a lot of decisions to be made as an Ebay sellers. It's important that you do what is best for your business and your bottom line. You might want to test offering returns BUT not free returns to see how it works for you. However, remember that you do NOT have to accept returns, free or otherwise, despite whatever pressure you might feel from Ebay.

Feedback: Feedback can be one of the most stressful parts of selling on Ebay for new sellers. Getting those first positive feedbacks is critical to gaining buyers' trust and increasing your sales.

I firmly believe in leaving feedback after a buyer has paid for their item. If the customer hasn't given me any trouble (they haven't asked a bunch of questions or been rude) and they have paid promptly for the item they bought, then they have fulfilled their part of the bargain and they deserve positive feedback. Some sellers refuse to leave feedback until they themselves have gotten it, but I believe it is simply the right thing to do to leave feedback first. As soon as I have printed the shipping label, I go back to "My Ebay" and leave the buyer positive feedback.

Something a lot of new sellers will do that I frown upon is to ask (sometimes beg) customers to leave them feedback. I remember when I first started selling on Ebay (back when sellers could leave customers negative feedback) that some sellers would leave a negative for anyone who asked them for feedback, just to spite them for asking. While sellers can no longer leave buyers negative feedback, the same annoyance for anyone asking for feedback still exists.

I personally cringe when someone asks me to leave them feedback. As I stated earlier, unless the buyer caused my problems, I always leave positive feedback, anyway; so usually the person asking has already gotten their feedback.

Many people will disagree with me, but I just advise NOT asking for feedback. As long as you are buying and/or selling within Ebay's terms, let the feedback come naturally. While I know this is hard to do when you are starting from zero and trying to build feedback, letting customers leave honest feedback without being hassled for it really is the best practice. Let Ebay nag the buyer for you as they will periodically send messages reminding customers to leave feedback.

Under Promise, Over Deliver: As I talked about earlier in this book, one of the best pieces of advice I read when starting my Ebay business was to under promise and over deliver. If you state in your Ebay listing that you ship in two days, ship in one. If you have an item that is in like-new condition, only state that it is in great condition. Exceeding your buyers' expectations will result in great feedback, which will encourage others to buy from you!

Blocking Bad Buyers: If you have had problems with a buyer, you can easily block them from buying anything from you again. Simply click on the "Site Map" link that is at the bottom of every Ebay page. Under the "Selling Activities" section is a "Block Bidder/Buyer List". Simply add the Ebay user name of the person you want to block and they will no longer be able to buy or bid on your items.

You can also block buyers with a history of problems in your listings under the "Buyer Requirements" section of all listings. I choose the minimum blocking requirements provided by Ebay to cut down on potential problems. While some bad buyers will still get through, you will at least be preventing those with strikes against them from causing you problems.

CHAPTER 8

TROUBLESHOOTING TIPS & TRICKS

Even if you follow all of the tips and tricks in this book, which are designed to avoid most customer problems, it's inevitable that you will occasionally run into issues when you are selling on Ebay. Fortunately, Ebay provides a number of safeguards to protect both buyers and sellers. You want to resolve all issues through Ebay's system of messaging and reporting; do not attempt to problem solve through direct email or by phone, as doing so will void any seller's protection you may be eligible for.

Filing an Unpaid Bidder Claim: Nothing is more frustrating than selling an item on Ebay only to have the buyer not pay. Fortunately, there are steps you can take to either get the customer to make payment or to recoup your fees and relist the item.

First of all, it's important to remember that Ebay gives buyers four days to pay. Therefore, you can't demand payment the next day. While you can change your Fixed Price listings to require immediate payment, this option doesn't work for auctions. There is no point in telling auction winners that they have to pay immediately as those are not Ebay's rule. Remember, Ebay is a TOOL you are using in your business. Ebay is NOT your business, so you have to follow THEIR rules.

After an auction ends, Ebay will notify the winner that they need to make payment. However, if they don't pay within an hour, I will then send the buyer an invoice. This is easy to do as it is an option in the drop-down menu next to the item in your "My Ebay" section. Usually the buyer will pay in a day or two. However, if by the third day I still haven't received payment, I then send a second invoice AND a message with a "friendly reminder" that their payment is due by the following day.

If you are confused about what day the buyer has until to pay, simply choose "Resolve a Problem" from the drop-down menu next to the item in "My Ebay". By then selecting the "I haven't received my payment" option, Ebay will tell you when you can file a claim.

If, after sending a second invoice and a message, I still haven't received payment, I will then open a claim. Ebay then contacts the buyer themselves to let them know that they need to make payment immediately or they will get an unpaid item strike. The vast majority of the time, this is enough to get the buyer to pay. However, they have four days from Ebay's warning to make payment. If after that additional four days you haven't gotten your money, you can close the claim case and recoup all of your listing and final value fees.

If a buyer ends up not paying and I have to file and then close a case, I then relist the item AND I block the buyer. I simply highlight and copy the buyer's Ebay screen name and go to the "Site Map" link that is at the bottom of all Ebay pages. From there, it's easy to find the "Add to My Blocked Buyers" link, where I simply paste in the name of the buyer and hit "save".

During this entire process, the only direct contact I make with the buyer is the ONE message reminding them that their payment is due. I don't message them every day. I don't message them telling them I'm filing a claim. And I don't message them that they've been blocked. I let Ebay handle all communication with the buyer, which they will do by sending them a message about the unpaid claim and warning them that they will get a strike if they don't submit payment.

Reporting Buyers: I always say that 99.9% of my Ebay customers are awesome, and that only .01% ever cause me problems. However, when someone is being mean or threatening online, it often feels like everyone is against you.

Fortunately, if someone is harassing you, you can report them to Ebay. Ebay is not only proactive when it comes to getting bad sellers off of the site, but in recent years, they have begun to crack down harder on bad buyers, too.

If someone has sent you an inappropriate message through the Ebay messaging system (trying to extort feedback or cussing at you), you can easily report them through the link provided in the "Marketplace Safety Tip" box under the message. Simply click on the "Report an inappropriate email" link. Ebay will then be able to see the message for themselves and take action.

Don't engage with a threatening buyer yourself; simply ignore them and report them to Ebay. I also take the step to block them so that they can't buy anything else from me. Again, by keeping all communication on Ebay's site, Ebay has a record of any threats or harassment, and they can take action on their end, which prevents you from having to further deal with problem customers.

Ebay Support: Ebay support is available by phone, although they don't make finding their number very easy! They first want you to sort through a list of Frequently Asked Questions to see if you can solve your problem that way.

At the very bottom of all Ebay pages are several links, including a "Contact us" link. When you click on "Contact us", you will be taken to a page where you can select from two tabs, "Find an answer" or "Contact Ebay". When you click on the "Contact Ebay" tab, you will be presented with a number of FAQ options, again in an effort to see if you can find the answer yourself. However, when you click any of these options, the next screen will have "Call Us" and Call Me" options on the left. Simply click which you prefer and follow the directions from there to speak with an Ebay representative by phone.

If you don't get the help you need from an Ebay representative, don't hesitate to hang up and call back again to speak with someone else. Ebay phone reps are basically call center workers with only on-screen directions to go by. While the first rep you speak with may not know how to find the answer to your problem, a more experienced rep might.

Privacy/Safety: While the internet offers a level of anonymity, when you are on Ebay, there are definitely some extra precautions you want to take. First and foremost is guarding your Ebay and PayPal log-in information. Change your passwords often, and make them a combination of letters, numbers and characters so that they will be nearly impossible to hack.

The only legitimate messages from Ebay and PayPal will come to you via the Ebay messaging system that you access when you are logged in. At the top of your "My Ebay" page are tabs, one of which is for messages. Ebay and PayPal do NOT send emails, although hackers do. A common email message says you need to click a link to reset your password or log in to your account. Never click on these email links, and do not give your Ebay or PayPal information to anyone claiming to be from the companies either by phone or email.

Keeping your home address private is another concern for Ebay sellers. I myself never worried too much about this until recently, when I finally got a P.O. Box so that I could make that my return mailing address for packages. Remember that your address will print out with your shipping label, so if you are sending out a lot of packages, you may want to make that address someplace other than home (such as your spouses' work or a P.O. Box). While this shouldn't be a huge concern (after all, people have been using their home addresses for years), it may be something you want to consider.

I have a designated email set up specifically for Ebay in which all Ebay and PayPal communications go through. I also guard my phone number, although some sellers do set up a number specifically for Ebay customers to call.

I also do not engage with customers outside of the Ebay system. Several times over the years, buyers have gotten a hold of my phone number and called my house. I simply delete these calls. I do the same with direct emails; I delete them without responding. If an Ebay customer wants to communicate with me, they need to contact me directly through Ebay.

CONCLUSION

Ebay is constantly changing and evolving. The feedback system is continually being revamped, and new features, such as Global Shipping, are always being added to the site. However, one thing remains the same: Good selling policies are the best way to ensure your Ebay success!

By utilizing the tips and tricks in this book, you will be doing everything in your power to increase your Ebay sales and avoid problems. Of course, having a product that customers want is the first step; but taking care of your buyers is just as important. Detailed listings, great pictures and stellar customer service are essential; as is utilizing all of the features Ebay has to offer.

Remember: Ebay is a TOOL you use in your business; it is not *your* business. Use the tips and tricks that I have provided to get the most out of the Ebay site, and you'll see your sales and bank account grow!

Selling on Ebay, while fun and profitable, is work. The harder you work, the more money you will make!

ABOUT THE AUTHOR

Ann Eckhart is a writer, blogger, YouTube creator, social media influencer, and Ebay seller based in Iowa. She has numerous books available about selling on Ebay as well as saving money and making money online. For more information, visit her website at AnnEckhart.com.